# BASIC JUDAISM

# BASIC JUDAISM

# MILTON STEINBERG

# BASIC JUDAISM

A Harvest Book
Harcourt Brace & Company
San Diego   New York   London

Requests for permission to make copies of
any part of the work should be mailed to:
Permissions Department,
Harcourt Brace & Company, 6277 Sea Harbor Drive,
Orlando, Florida 32887-6777.

ISBN 0-15-610698-1 (Harvest: pbk.)

Printed in the United States of America

First Harvest edition 1975

DD EE FF GG

# CONTENTS

## V. THE GOOD LIFE

## VI. ISRAEL AND THE NATIONS

## VII. PRACTICES

# VIII. LAW

# IX. INSTITUTIONS

# X. WORLD-TO-COME

# EPILOGUE

# PREFACE

This is a book about the Jewish religion. Not about Jews, or Jewish problems, or Jewish culture, or Zionism, but about those beliefs, ideals, and practices which make up the historic Jewish faith.

In writing it I have tried to be as concise as possible, and as simple as a complex and often subtle subject matter would allow. At the same time I have not been so concerned with brevity and simplicity as to confine myself to a mere cataloguing of facts. This book is interpretive as well as descriptive.

Always, however, I have striven to be objective, to suppress my private viewpoint, to depict Judaism as it is, and, where Jews differ in their construction of it, to give each party a fair hearing. But while I am neutral, at least in these pages, as among contending Jewish sects, whether traditionalist or nontraditionalist, whether Orthodox, Conservative, or Reform, I am not neutral on Judaism itself. I am a professing Jew whose faith is a matter of heart as well as head, of ardor no less than conviction. Of this enthusiasm I could not make a secret if I would; I would not if I could.

Like any author I welcome any reader. But I have intended *Basic Judaism* for three groups of people especially.

It is addressed in the first instance to believing Jews in the hope that, finding in it a lucid and ordered formulation of their faith, they may be encouraged to live that faith the more consistently and forthrightly.

It is directed equally to that large body of heretofore indifferent Jews who, whether in response to pressures from without or voids within, are groping to establish rapport with the Jewish Tradition, standing at the synagogue's doors "heart in, head out." *Basic Judaism* is not a missionary text. It is declaratory, not exhortatory. But in that fact may lie its usefulness for these wavering Jews. Here, so to speak, is the faith with which they must, if they can, come to terms.

This book is designed last of all for those many non-Jews who happen to be curious about Judaism. The Christian in quest of an objective understanding of the Jewish religion is not a person to be envied. To be sure, he will find books aplenty dealing with his theme. But if they are of Christian authorship they will pretty generally present Judaism only in so far as it bears on the emergence of Christianity or solely for the purpose of contrasting it with its daughter faith, almost always to its disadvantage. And if they have been written by Jews they will tend to be excessively detailed and to assume a larger body of background information than the typical non-Jew possesses. Even worse, they are quite likely to be slanted in favor of some special viewpoint, or else to be preoccupied with confusing and, to an outsider, irrelevant sectarian differences.

What has long been needed is a book on Judaism, written from within Judaism and hence sympathetic to it, concerned with it for its own sake and not as a foil for something else, unencumbered with details and as free as possible from doctrinal and ritualistic dissensions. For only from such a book can the undecided Jew and the inquiring non-Jew come to see Judaism as believing Jews see it, to comprehend why it has elicited from them such intense and sustained loyalty, and proved so mighty a force in their lives and through them in human affairs generally.

To these purposes this book is dedicated. That it shall realize all of them and in their completeness is more than I expect. It is my hope only that it will achieve some of them at least in part. As for the residue of goals destined to be missed and of intentions fated to be fulfilled but fractionally —there remains the consoling epigram of the ancient Sages of Israel:

"Not thine to finish the task, but neither art thou free to exempt thyself from it."

# BASIC JUDAISM

## I. THE NATURE OF JUDAISM

The word "Judaism" has two distinct and equally legitimate meanings. Sometimes it denotes a full civilization; the total actualities, past and present, of the historic group of human beings known as the Jewish people. In this significance, it embraces secular as well as sacred elements; for example, the love songs of medieval Hebrew poets, the folk music and dance of East European Jewries, social institutions of all sorts, and much else.

Just as properly, "Judaism" may stand for something more limited: the spiritual aspect of that civilization; in sum, for the Jewish religion.

It is in this latter sense that we shall use the word in this book.

The Jewish religion, however, even when isolated from the rest of the civilization, is far from being simple and homogeneous.

No less than seven strands weave together to make it up:

1. A doctrine concerning God, the universe, and man;
2. A morality for the individual and society;
3. A regimen of rite, custom, and ceremony;
4. A body of law;

3

5. A sacred literature;
6. Institutions through which the foregoing find expression;
7. The people, Israel—central strand out of which and about which the others are spun.

Now it is possible in the mind to disentangle these threads. One may say, "Let us consider the doctrine apart from the ethic, or both aside from the literature, or all away from the people which created and sustains them." One can think these things but not do them.

First, because, where the cords are actually distinct, they have knotted so tightly under the wear and tear of centuries that no amount of picking can pull them apart.

And second, because the unity of Judaism is more than that of a knot. Most of the seemingly distinct threads are in reality different organs of the same creature, animated by a common spirit, reaching into and penetrating one another, no more to be isolated than the parts of a body.

For—and this is the crux of the matter—Judaism is an organism; the fabric of its weaving is alive.

## 2. THE TIME FACTOR

Judaism has four thousand years of history behind it and in it.

That history is too long and involved to be recounted here. Nor is it our immediate concern. Yet it is so much a factor in the Jewish religion that we shall need, if not a knowledge of it, at least some sense of its color and sweep.

The most direct approach to the Jewish past is through

the people who made it. Let us then consider them in their generations.

Together they make a strange, impressive company, living out a strange, impressive destiny.

There are among them—

—Semites of long before the time of Abraham; those who built great civilizations in the valleys of the Tigris and Euphrates and those who as nomads roamed the Arabian wastes.

—The Patriarchs, adrift almost four millennia ago in the land of Canaan, heirs to city and desert alike; forefathers of a peculiar people, of its insights and values.

—The man Moses, emancipator of a people and its law-giver, who dwarfs the mountain on which he stands.

—Palestinian peasants, hesitating between two ways—the stern traditions of their ancestors and the soft, often corrupt practices of the Amorites, Canaanites, and Hittites among whom they dwelt.

—The Prophets, boldest of all pioneers and discoverers in the realm of the spirit:

Nathan and Elijah who rebuked kings for deeds of oppression.

Amos, shepherd and trimmer of sycamore trees, who proclaimed the universality of God and the primacy of justice in His service.

Hosea who, out of the capacity for forgiveness he found in himself, leaped to the dazzling vision of a God inexhaustible in mercy.

Isaiah who espied design in history and defined the climax toward which it moves: God's Kingdom of universal peace and equity.

And Jeremiah and Micah and Ezekiel and Habakkuk and Jonah . . .

—Psalmists who sang so movingly of God that the worship not only of the Synagogue but of the Church and Mosque as well echoes them to this day.

—Sages of the days of the Second Temple who composed or collected words of wisdom, the Books of Proverbs and Ecclesiastes, and ben Sira and what is perhaps the most superb single literary work of all time, the Book of Job.

—Hellenized Jews of the Greco-Roman age—Philo of Alexandria, for example—who synthesized the traditions of their people with the wisdom of Greece.

—Teachers of the three centuries before and the five after the beginning of the Common Era, builders of those treasure-houses of piety, idealism, and Jewish lore: the *Mishnah*, the Babylonian and Palestinian *Talmuds*, the *Midrashim*. These are the men who next after the prophets did most to fashion Judaism in its historic guise; this is the group that we shall have in mind when we allude, as we shall so often, to "the rabbis."

—The Nazarene and his disciples who, though they did not directly affect the Judaism they professed and practiced, yet remade the Western World and so exerted a circuitous influence on their own people and faith.

—Commentators and expositors of Scripture and rabbinic literature, scholars in Jewish theology and law, of all times and places, who systematized a vast tradition, realized its potentialities, and enriched it out of their own souls.

—The poets, grammarians, exegetes, scientists, translators, and historians of the Golden Age of medieval Spanish Jewry.

—Philosophers harmonizing the Hebraic world-view with

the dominant metaphysical systems of their respective eras, from the Platonic and Aristotelian to the neo-Kantian and Pragmatist.

—Kabbalists and other mystics in quest of direct and immediate knowledge of the One behind the many, of the Real behind the seeming.

—Moralists of diverse lands and eras meditating on the good life and how it is best to be achieved.

—Those late medieval pietists, the *Hasidim*, intoxicated with God and with the joy of existence.

—The *Maskilim*, the "Enlighteners" of the eighteenth and nineteenth centuries; who breached Ghetto walls so that the tides of modernity might surge in and the Jewish spirit, after a half millennium's confinement, might flow out.

—The historians and lexicographers of the last one hundred and fifty years, dedicated to scientific research into the Jewish past, who have retrieved so much of Judaism from the ruin wrought by time, persecution, and neglect.

—Reformers of many kinds and fashions at work during the nineteenth and twentieth centuries on the adaptation of the historic Jewish way to modern circumstances; their opponents, the traditionalists, resisting change as sacrilegious or perilous or both.

—Those who today build the Jewish homeland in Palestine and so make possible the brilliant renaissance of Hebrew culture now in process there.

—The innumerable martyrs of all generations from the first to the latest whose devotion even unto death has sanctified Judaism.

—And the myriads upon myriads of obscure people— neither prophets nor rabbis nor philosophers nor poets nor scholars nor martyrs—who lived, died, and, having left no name behind, are now swallowed up in a vast anonymity, but who no less than "the men of fame" loved and served the spiritual heritage of their people. Their imprint, too, though without signature, may be deciphered in Judaism as it now is.

For, of the total Jewish enterprise in regard to those who participated in it, no matter when or in what role or measure, there may be said what the High Holyday liturgy says of the Book of Life: "The seal of every man's hand is in it."

### 3. THE MEANING OF "BASIC"

Does the notion *basic* Judaism make sense?

Here is Judaism, a composite of seven elements, the work of many hands, the product of varied times and conditions.

Can one generalize about an entity so heterogeneous and long-lived, let alone determine what is essential to it and what accidental, what abiding and what permanent?

In other words, in setting out to describe *basic* Judaism, are we undertaking to catch a will-o'-the-wisp, something to which, given the nature of Judaism, there can be no corresponding reality?

Not at all! Many beings are complex and forever involved in change but still exhibit fundamental characters over which time and its vicissitudes have no dominion.

A person lives, grows, is transformed by years and circumstance, and yet maintains all along a continuing identity. A sameness of body binds together the baby, the mature man, the gray-beard. There is an even greater and more consequential identity of character and soul, a basic personality-structure, which persists from childhood to the grave, making a oneness of a life.

So with Judaism. Its seven strands, for all their twining and interweaving, make a steady design which is visible no matter at what point one cuts across them. To be sure, there are differences from place to place, sometimes so· marked as to obscure the sameness. But whether obvious or hidden, the sameness is always there.

This then is what we mean by *basic* Judaism. It is the common denominator of all the elements of Judaism through all its history, the characteristics which have persisted in childhood and maturity alike, the traits which have gone on and on, the design that is discernible no matter where a cross section is taken.

#### 4. TRADITIONALISTS AND MODERNISTS

Judaism exhibits a unified and continuing spiritual pattern throughout its history. Except for its beginnings at one extreme and its most recent phases at the other.

Thus, in its earliest stages, in the days before the great prophets, it reveals the pattern only faintly, more as a promise than an actuality.

At the hither end of the Jewish career the classic design blurs again, or to put it more accurately, splits apart, unraveling into two major variants with all sorts of splinter deviations in between.

The modern world is the cutting edge against which this division has worked itself.

For several hundred years, up to the French Revolution, the bulk of the Jews of Europe were isolated quite effectively from the rest of mankind. Confined to Ghettos, they lived a life almost entirely their own. Then in the eighteenth and nineteenth centuries they were "emancipated"; that is to say, made free to live where they pleased, enter any occupations they preferred, participate in the political and cultural life of their native lands as they desired.

This experience was one of release and liberation. But it was also a shock. It not only transformed their social condition; it shook them intellectually and emotionally. For abroad in this strange new world were strange new ideas, scientific, philosophical, and moral, which seemed to challenge historic Jewish beliefs and ideals.

A Jewish revolution as well as a French began on July 14, 1789. Continuing to this day, it is the cause and occasion for the appearance of two distinct versions of the Jewish religion.

There are those Jews who refuse to be moved in even the slightest degree from the faith, morality, and practices of their fathers. These are the *strict* traditionalists.

Others, though, have decided that Judaism needs to be adapted to modern ideas and circumstances. These Jews are also traditionalists. The faith they cherish, the principles they pursue, the rituals they observe, the synagogues they frequent—all derive from historic Judaism and are permeated with its values. But they have departed, whether much or little, consciously or inadvertently, from the old pattern. They might be described as "modernist-traditionalists," were the phrase not so cumbersome. Let us call them simply "modernists," understanding all along that they are traditionalists, also.

Accordingly, whenever we speak of Judaism without labels and tags, we shall be talking of those points on which both traditionalists and modernists think alike. On other occasions, however, we shall have to draw distinctions between different versions of the classic design.

We shall be doing more of the former than the latter. I say this so explicitly because having prepared the reader for disagreements I would not have him exaggerate either their number or their depth.

The two groups, traditionalist and modernist, have more in common than apart. Their viewpoints make up not two religions but variants of one.

# II

## CONCLUSIONS

### I. THE END OF THE MATTER

Long ago, as long ago as a full two thousand years, when Judaism though still young was already old enough to have a well-defined character, a number of attempts were made to catch that character in some terse formula.

One such effort was that of Hillel, a Palestinian sage and saint who lived just before the beginning of the Christian era.

Of him it is related that on being challenged by a pagan to tell all about Judaism in the few moments during which a man might stand on one foot, he responded:

"That which is hurtful to thee do not to thy neighbor. This is the whole doctrine. The rest is commentary. Now go forth and learn."

In the second century Rabbi Akiba son of Joseph found the "great principle" of Judaism in the commandment laid down in Leviticus:

"Thou shalt love thy neighbor as thyself."

His contemporary and colleague, Simeon son of Azzai, put forth as an alternative "great principle" the verse from Genesis: "This is the book of the generations of man. In the day that God created man, *in the likeness of God made He him.*" So Simeon indicated that more fundamental even

12

than the love of man is the awareness of his kinship with Deity.

But it is in a homily by Simlai, a rabbi of the third century, that we find what is perhaps the most ingenious and thoroughgoing of all ventures at reducing the Jewish faith to its essence.

Rabbi Simlai taught:

"Six hundred and thirteen commandments were imparted to Moses—three hundred and sixty-five of which were prohibitions, answering to the number of the days of the year, and two hundred and forty-eight positive precepts, corresponding to the number of members in the human body.

"Then came David and reduced them to eleven, even as it is written (Psalms XV):

Lord, who shall sojourn in Thy tabernacle?
Who shall dwell on Thy holy mountain?
He that walketh uprightly, and worketh righteousness,
And speaketh truth in his heart;
That hath no slander upon his tongue,
Nor doeth evil to his fellow
Nor taketh up a reproach against his neighbor;
In whose eyes a vile person is despised,
But he honoreth them that fear the Lord;
He that sweareth to his own hurt and breaketh not his word;
He that putteth not out his money on interest,
Nor taketh a bribe against the innocent.
He that doeth these things shall never be moved.

"Then came Isaiah and reduced them to six, even as it is written (Isaiah XXXIII: 15):

He that walketh righteously, and speaketh uprightly;
He that despiseth the gain of oppressions,
That shaketh clear his hands from laying hold on bribes,
That stoppeth his ears from hearing of blood
And shutteth his eyes from looking upon evil.

"Then came Micah and reduced them to three, even as it is written (Micah VI:8):

It hath been told thee, O man, what is good,
And what the Lord doth require of thee:
Only to do justly, and to love mercy, and to walk humbly
   with thy God.

"Then came Isaiah once more and reduced them to two, as it is said (Isaiah LVI:1):

Thus saith the Lord:
Keep ye justice, and do righteousness.

"Then came Amos and reduced them to one, as it is said (Amos V:4):

Seek ye Me, and live."

Rabbi Nahman the son of Isaac (a Babylonian scholar of the second or third generation after Rabbi Simlai) suggests as an alternative conclusion:

"Then came the prophet Habakkuk and reduced the commandments to one, which one is the verse (Habakkuk II:4):

The righteous shall live by his faith."

The foregoing were of course not the only attempts in Jewish history at distilling and crystallizing the essence of Judaism. They are, however, representative and sufficient to establish that basic to Judaism is a twofold affirmation concerning God on the one hand and man on the other; the former being that a man shall seek to know God, love Him, revere Him, and do His will; the latter that a man shall love his fellow men also, dealing with them in righteousness and mercy.

What is more, the duality of the attitudes as to God and man is more seeming than real. For to Judaism one love is the obverse and consequence of the other. Piety toward God is meaningless unless it induces compassion toward human beings. (Can one genuinely revere the Creator and not His creation, the Spirit but not Its manifestation?) By the same token, every act of righteousness and mercy reveals the Divinity resident within the doer and implies the recognition of an equal Divinity touching the person done by.

The simultaneous love of God and man: here is Judaism's first postulate and final inference, its point of departure and its destination, the root of it and its fruitage.

Whereupon a question suggests itself: Are we perhaps so soon done with our enterprise? In the preface, it will be recalled, we defined our goal as an understanding of the fundamentals of the Jewish religion. But is not that purpose already achieved? And if so, is not this book completed with its very first pages?

In a sense, yes. Everything of Judaism to be considered from this moment forward will derive from and converge on the principle we have already formulated. Yet, on other scores, it is clear that the end of the matter must still be far, far off.

Consider the fact that Judaism is not the only communion to set the love of God and man as its key motif. Christianity and Mohammedanism, religions born of Judaism and fashioned in appreciable degree after its image, rest on the same foundation and reach toward the same pinnacle. Nevertheless Judaism is quite distinct from either of its daughter faiths. Obviously, then, there must be more to our story than has yet been disclosed.

Again, we have in actuality learned less about Judaism than we may at first surmise. We know of it that it is concerned with God and man, but we are still ignorant of how it conceives either. All we have acquired so far is a pair of words, with no hint as to the actualities for which they stand.

Still again, we have been informed that Judaism sets certain objectives before man. But we have been afforded no notion of the path it expects him to travel to reach them. Yet the way he goes may determine what he shall be and what he shall find at his destination. Whence it follows that we grasp little of Judaism by the knowledge of its ends alone; we must comprehend its means and methods also.

Finally, all truth, all ideals, if they are more than verbal, strive after embodiment, living only to the degree in which they attain it.

Democracy requires translation into concrete institutions and practices. Nor does one know it if his understanding is of theory only.

The theme in the mind of the composer struggles toward incarnation, spinning forth variations and weaving orchestrations about itself. Nor is the composition to be possessed by the acquisition of its major motifs.

A person is a far richer being than his ideas and convictions, no matter how various and dominant they are. A person is also flesh and blood, memory and hope.

By the same token the Jewish religion, like any other, must be more, infinitely more, than its core doctrine.

All of which is no doubt what Hillel meant in his closing words to the impatient pagan. For, having formulated the corner stone principle of Judaism, having characterized all else as commentary, he nevertheless insisted that the commentary be mastered also.

"Go forth and learn," he said.

## I. THE TORAH-BOOK

It has been suggested that the spirit of a religion is most readily to be caught in the architecture it evokes, that from Gothic cathedrals to Quaker meeting houses churches reflect and manifest the faiths that have created them.

By such a criterion, Judaism at first glance would seem to have no character in particular. Synagogues are of almost every conceivable style and ornamentation. Nor do they invariably exhibit even such conventional symbols as the Tables of the Commandments, the six-pointed Shield of David, or the many-branched candelabra. The fact is that Jews have been too much on the move and too harried in the process to evolve a distinctive pattern for their places of worship.

Synagogues, however, for all their diversity do have one feature in common. Every synagogue possesses, enshrines, and makes accessible at least one copy, in scroll form, of the book known as the Torah. With this book go almost unfailingly certain appurtenances: robes and adornments with which it is draped, an Ark or cabinet in which it is housed, a lectern from which it is read, and an ever-burning lamp reminiscent of that which illuminated the Tabernacle and the Temple in ancient times, but symbolic equally of the unquenchable light of the book.

Not only does every synagogue contain this book; it is primarily by virtue of its presence, together with that of a congregation, that a synagogue is a synagogue, that is to say, a place set apart for Jewish worship.

And here, in the role assigned to a book, we have that clue to the spirit and structure of Judaism which in other communions is supplied by the architecture of their churches.

Judaism is a *book* religion, deriving from, centering about, and making explicit the contents of a sacred document.

## 2. THE BOOK AS BOOK

Like other texts of great consequence in human affairs, the Torah is, so to speak, more than itself and its actual contents. In the next chapter we shall see what that "more" may be. But first to the book *qua* book.

As a physical object the Torah is a parchment sheet, or rather a succession of parchment sheets sewn together breadthwise and rolled about two wooden poles so as to make twin cylinders. These sheets contain the Hebrew original, handinscribed and painstakingly edited for absolute accuracy, of the first five books of Scripture, the Mosaic books, Genesis, Exodus, Leviticus, Numbers, and Deuteronomy.

In form the Torah is a narrative, an account of events from the creation of the world to the death of Moses. Between these limits it describes the origins of the nations of the earth and, with especial attention, the beginnings of the people of Israel, the lives of the Patriarchs, the enslavement of the Jews in Egypt, their deliverance and the revelations of God's will which came to them in the wilderness of Sinai.

But the Torah is much more than a narrative.

Among other things it sets forth, if not systematically at least most vividly, a doctrine concerning a one and universal God: the Creator of all things, the Lawgiver, Liberator, and Redeemer of men.

It outlines an ethic of justice and loving-kindness. Sometimes these moral principles flare into white incandescence as in the Decalogue or the Holiness Code of Leviticus XIX. More generally they are assumed and implied. In one guise or another, not a line in the text is devoid of them.

It prescribes rituals, holy days, and festive seasons, together with pertinent forms of worship and observance.

It promulgates a code of law, ecclesiastical, civil, and criminal.

It ordains institutions, religious, domestic, social, philanthropic, and political.

It propounds a conception of the Jewish people as a "kingdom of priests and a holy nation," through whom all the families of the earth are to be blessed.

Beyond all these, it constitutes a monumental literary achievement. It was a superb stylist who wrote the thundering first chapter of Genesis. An uncannily expert story-teller unwound the poignant, haunting story of Joseph. And no mere talented rhetorician composed the farewell orations of Moses or conjured up the picture of the dying prophet seeing the promised land from afar.

Such is the Torah-Book.

To different people it means different things.

To the perceptive unbeliever it represents at the least a

literary masterpiece and the earliest clear formulation of the ethic of justice and compassion.

To the religious man of any Western communion, this is the book of the generations of his beliefs, the seed from which have sprung the theological and moral premises by which he lives.

But to the professing Jew, the Torah-Book is all these and infinitely more. It is not only a source of what he is as a Jew and religious person, it is much of the substance as well.

### 3. THE TORAH-TRADITION

Torah as a specific book is Torah only in its most restricted sense.

There are broader connotations to the concept, and other significances still more comprehensive than these. In their aggregate and latitude they constitute a whole world of ideas and values.

Into this universe of discourse, the quickest entrance is by way of a bit of etymology, that of the word "Torah" itself.

Torah is a Hebrew noun derived from the verb which means "to guide" or "to teach." Quite simply and literally therefore it stands for "guidance" or "teaching" or, to use a word of Latin origin, "doctrine."

Once Torah is so rendered, its broader connotations virtually spell themselves out. Obviously the Teaching did not cease with Moses or the books ascribed to him. The prophets carried it on, and so did the poets and sages who composed Psalms, Proverbs, and Job. Hence, the latter books of Scripture, while not Torah in letter, are very much Torah in spirit.

But so, too, are the writings of the classical rabbinic age (from the third century before the Common Era to the fifth century after). In these works, commonly described as Talmudic, the teaching was consolidated, expounded, and advanced.

But commentators on the Bible and rabbinic literature, the moralists and philosophers of all times down to our own —they have unfolded the Teaching still further.

So in the end, under this wide envisagement, Torah becomes everything which has its roots in the Torah-Book, which is consistent with its outlook, which draws forth its implications, and which realizes its potentialities.

Torah in sum is all the vastness and variety of the Jewish Tradition.

To Jews throughout history, Torah, both the Book and the Tradition, has been incalculably precious and of spiritual import beyond all comparison.

Now, obviously, the incalculable cannot be calculated, nor the incomparable compared. Any effort then at describing the full meaning of Torah for committed Jews is foredoomed to failure. Yet the attempt must be ventured. For without at least some notion of the dynamic centrality of this concept among Jewish beliefs and values one does not so much as begin to comprehend them.

Let the great men of Torah then speak concerning it, those who, being closest to it and knowing it best, can be most articulate about it. And from their words we shall be able to form some estimates of its impact on the individual and the group.

To the Book of Deuteronomy Torah is the life and good which is set before man as an alternative to death and evil;

at the same time it is Israel's wisdom and understanding in the eyes of the nations.

To the Prophet it is the water for which all men thirst, the bread for which they starve—which is yet dispensed without silver or price.

To the Psalmist it is the light in which he sees light, or alternatively the spiritual sustenance whose taste is sweeter than honey and the drippings of the honeycomb.

To a Rabbi of ancient days it is something to be delved into further and further, since all things are in it; something over which a man may grow gray and old, never stirring from its contemplation, knowing that he can have no better pursuit or rule.

To medieval Jews in their Ghettos it is, by the testimony of a folk-song, a treasure better than all worldly goods.

To the modern Hebrew poet, Bialik, it is a great flame kindled on high altars in olden days.

And to all generations of Jews from Isaiah on it is the word of the Lord destined in the end to regenerate man and society.

## 4. TORAH——TRADITIONALIST VIEW

Torah, the bond uniting religious Jews, is also the theme of their most fundamental disagreement, the continental divide, as it were, at which traditionalist and modernist begin their divergence.

The basic distinction between the two viewpoints is this:

Traditionalists believe the whole Torah to be God-revealed, therefore unimpeachably true and good throughout.

Modernists hold that truth and goodness are to be found in the Torah, and that to the extent of their presence it is God-inspired.

To traditionalists the entire Torah-Book, every word, every letter, was imparted by God either directly to the whole people of Israel at Mount Sinai or indirectly through Moses. The fact of revelation is decisive. It is a guarantee of absolute validity, intellectual and moral.

But revelation, according to the traditionalists, does not exhaust itself in the Torah-Book. It suffuses the writings of the prophets after Moses, overflows into the rest of Scripture, thence into classical Talmudic literature; thence again, though in diminishing degree, into later rabbinic writings. In other words, the mainstream of the Tradition everywhere possesses something of the authority of the Torah-Book— much in the same fashion as inferences in logic, carry over, if only they be drawn accurately, the authority and certainty of the premises from which they are drawn. Or to put the point as does the Talmud itself: "Whatsoever any earnest scholar will innovate in the future, lo this was already spoken at Sinai."

From this postulate, that the Torah-Tradition like the Torah-Book is of divine inspiration (though not so absolutely), significant conclusions follow.

One is that Judaism cannot be susceptible to consequential change.

After all, God is not man. When He speaks it is fully and finally, in freedom from the human necessity of correcting Himself, editing an utterance, or pinning on afterthoughts. Judaism was complete and perfect at Sinai.

As for the historical growth through which the Tradition seems to have passed, this is basically illusion. The prophets, sages, and rabbis neither modified it in essence nor added aught to its substance. All they did was to recapitulate it in fresh idioms or to give it timely applications. A truth, however, is not altered—and certainly not enlarged—by being couched in one phraseology rather than another, just as a distance is neither extended nor contracted when it is translated from feet into inches. So, under all the restatements, Judaism has persisted as one and the same from Moses to our day.

Of divine authorship, Judaism cannot be subject to amendment by man. What mortal mind dare venture improvements on what God wrought at Sinai? What new truth or novel circumstance can possibly arise, unforeseen by Providence, to necessitate putting patches on revelation?

Does this mean that by traditionalist lights Judaism is altogether unbending and eternally immutable? Not quite. Some measure of flexibility inheres in it. It is always susceptible to reinterpretation; it may even be suspended in some of its provisions should a crisis arise to require so drastic a step. Both powers, to construe and to take emergency measures, belong to that "earnest scholar," concerning whom we have just quoted the Talmud. What is more, they are his and his colleagues' not by supererogation but by explicit statement of the Torah, which ordains: "If there arise a matter too hard for thee in judgment . . . thou shalt come unto the priests the Levites and unto the judge that shall be in those days . . . and thou shalt observe to do according to all that they shall teach thee."

Besides, at least some portion of doctrine and practice commonly accepted in Judaism represents no more than current but disputable interpretation of Torah, or established custom, or even private preference.

Judaism then is neither altogether rigid nor eternally unchanging. But the free play allowed by reinterpretation is not overly extensive and the right to issue emergency decrees has always been used sparingly. Constancy, then, despite changing times and circumstances, is a major characteristic of Torah in the view of the traditionalist and under his hands.

Last of all, to traditionalism the Torah is the first, last, and always reliable test of the goodness or truth of anything. Any proposition which contravenes the Tradition must be false, no matter how impressive the argument marshaled in its support. Any moral principle that is out of harmony with the Teaching must be of an imperfect rule, though it give every appearance of being wise and expedient.

This is not to say that reason and experience are worthless, or that philosophy, science, and naturalistic morality discharge no useful functions. On the contrary they occupy a large place in man's scheme and God's.

They are indispensable first of all in that they help to illuminate the dark places of Torah, to resolve its occasional seeming self-contradictions. Too, they supply the technical skills necessary for its practical application. Finally they equip men with a wide variety of insights and values which are fully legitimate and desirable, for all that they are (strictly speaking) irrelevant to Torah.

The traditionalist then bids philosophers and scientists a sincere *Godspeed* as they set forth to their business. Yet he is confident of the conclusions at which they will arrive if only they think long enough and hard enough, at least those of their conclusions which bear on virtue and happiness. Are not those conclusions written out for him in the Torah?

His, then, is the assurance of one who knows the answer to a riddle while others are struggling to work it out; who has read the last act of a drama and is therefore assured, even in its tensest moments, of a happy ending.

The ancient rabbis were wont to speak of some persons

as "acquiring eternity in one instant." So they characterized those who vindicate their entire lives in one heroic decision. Intellectually speaking, the Jewish traditionalist is in such a case.

He makes a single but tremendous act of faith; he posits a lone but gigantic postulate. He affirms that the Tradition is divinely inspired throughout. Thereafter only one truth is possible for him; only one way is open on which he can walk.

### 5. TORAH——MODERNIST VIEW

The modernist approaches Torah from diametrically the opposite direction.

To him the first criterion of the truth of a proposition or of the validity of a principle is not its conformity with the Tradition but its consonance with reason and experience. Far from judging all things by the standard of Torah, he tests Torah against the standards by which he judges everything else. And only in so far as Torah passes muster does he accept it as authoritative.

This momentous distinction between modernist and traditionalist stems from an even more basic difference: over the susceptibility of Judaism to fundamental change.

The modernist has been persuaded by the biological and social sciences that the law of change is universal and that Judaism is no exception to it; that it is no fixed and constant entity as the traditionalist holds but the end product of a long and still continuing growth.

Even the Torah-Book, according to the modernist, did not come into being all at one time, as the work of the single hand of Moses. To the contrary it achieved its familiar shape and dimensions only as the result of an evolutionary process. The typical modernist in other words follows higher criticism in the conclusion that the Torah text as we now have it is a composite of several documents done by diverse authors and sewn into unity by some unknown editor or editors.

These documents furthermore are not equally mature. Some, generally the earliest, are heavily weighted with the folk-lore of the ancient Jews, their rudimentary science and sometimes naive notions of God and morality. Others are consistently on the highest plane.

To be sure, even the most rudimentary passages often set forth or imply spiritual verities of the first magnitude. The universe may not have been created in six days as is asserted by the Torah, but in the eyes of religious people it remains the work of Spirit. Man may not have come into being after the fashion portrayed in Genesis, but that he is God's handiwork abides a point of faith. Perhaps there never was a universal flood, at least not in man's time or beyond the flat-lands of Mesopotamia, but who in the twentieth century will deny that by their collective sins men can precipitate catastrophes from which only righteousness can deliver them?

What is important then about the Torah-Book is not that it is all factual but that even where it is not it is still meaningful. What is even more important is that though it contains much of the primitive, it contains also the full-ripened insights which grew from these beginnings.

The modernist therefore is an eclectic about the Torah, regarding some passages with greater reverence than others and proving all alike on the double touchstone of reason and experience.

What goes for the Torah-Book applies even more closely

to the rest of Scripture and to the Tradition in its later phases. The modernist accepts these not because he assumes in advance that they are beyond the peradventure of doubt and criticism; but because, striving so steadily after truth and goodness, they achieve them so often and in such extraordinary degree.

This is the Tradition as the modernist sees it: the creation not of a miraculous and supernatural event but of a natural unfolding, the record left by a particular people of its pilgrimage out of darkness to clarity and compassion.

But if the Tradition be not self-validating, if it must be approved by reason and experience, what is its authority for the modernist? Why does he not take recourse to reason and experience directly?

Part of the answer is undoubtedly the reverence for the Tradition inculcated in childhood, ancestral pieties, sentiment, habit, group loyalties. The core of it, however, is another, deeper consideration.

To the modernist the Tradition has authority not because it obviates an appeal to naturalistic sources but because it gives so full a report of what men found out when they made just such an appeal, when they applied their heads and hearts to the deepest questions of human existence. The Tradition preserves the speculations of multitudes of rationalists, the accounts of countless mystics, the conclusions of innumerable persons plumbing their own souls, the balance sheets of lives beyond calculation, and a protracted experience with the ideas of faith as to their long range tenability and their power to humanize the heart. Not something different from reason and experience but a titanic compendium of their findings, this is the Tradition.

"But where," one may ask, "is God in this concept?"

"Where," the modernist responds, "is He not? Is not God the power behind all human aspiration and attainment, the impulse driving men toward the good, the true, and the beautiful? Who other than He stirred the remotest generations of Israel with a nameless discontent? Who impelled all the fumbling achievements of this people through the centuries? Who possessed the souls of its prophets? Who made judicious the hearts of its sages? Who rendered intransigent the spirits of it martyrs? Who, save One?"

Torah remains a revelation in the eyes of the modernist; but in general, not in detail, in its high climax rather than its lower reaches, in its directions though not necessarily in each step.

Manifestly, an abyss separates the modernist from the traditionalist in their respective views of Torah.

But an abyss, no matter how broad and deep, is a cleft in the earth's surface. The walls to either side will be of similar composition; they will be joined by a common ground below and may be even further united by a bridge from above.

So, though the traditionalist and the modernist differ over Torah, both revere it, each after his own understanding and fashion; both look to it for guidance and inspiration.

And both stand on the same ground, are made of the same stuff, and surmount their disagreements in arches of shared purpose.

# GOD

## IV

## I. CREEDS

For the past one hundred and fifty years a quiet debate has been going on among Jewish theologians over the question: Are there dogmas in Judaism? Does it have a set of beliefs, authoritatively formulated, which the individual Jew must accept if he wishes to be a communicant in good standing in the Jewish religion? Or to put it otherwise, is there anything in the Tradition akin, let us say, to the Apostles, Nicene, and Athanasian Creeds of the Roman Catholic church, the Augsburg Confession of Lutheranism, or the Westminster Confession of Presbyterianism?

Since some Jewish scholars answer these inquiries to one effect and others to another, it might be well were we to allow each side to present its case. Let us then hear first from those who deny the presence in Judaism of a binding creed, then from their opponents, and finally from a moderator who stands midway between the two positions.

The nondogmatists speak:

We hold that Judaism cannot be a creedal religion, and that for three reasons:

First, if Judaism has dogmas, where are they? Why were they never formulated officially, not even in the days when authoritative bodies existed capable of formulating and imposing them? Why, for example, did the Sanhedrin during seven hundred years of spiritual predominance never publish a set of articles of Jewish faith?

Second, no draft of the Jewish creed attempted by any individual has ever won universal acceptance, not even the Thirteen Principles of Faith drawn up by Moses Maimonides, the undisputed master of all medieval Jewish theologians. For though at the present time most orthodox Jews view the Maimonidean creed with great reverence, every article in it has been challenged by someone or another, and more than an occasional orthodox Jew is a critic of it to this day.

Third, Jews cannot share a set of dogmas for the very simple but compelling reason that they have never been of one mind on theological matters. The Bible itself discloses diversities in religious outlook. The sages of the Talmud are surprisingly variegated in their convictions. Some are rationalists, some mystics; some are transcendentalists who regard God as apart from the world, others are immanentists; some take the biblical account of the revelation at Sinai with utmost literalness, at least one treats it as an allegory. Doctrinal difference has always been the rule among professing Jews; it is the rule more sweepingly in modern times.

From which it follows relentlessly that there is no specific Jewish creed. Q.E.D.

The dogmatists speak:

To say that Judaism has no dogmas is absurd.

First, it is to assert of the Jewish religion that it stands for nothing in particular, that it is a jellyfish of a faith.

Second, if Judaism has no distinctive convictions, what

kept the Jews together all through their long and stormy history? What was it for which Jewish martyrs died?

Third, Judaism has from time to time taken firm stands against ideas current in the world about itself. Thus in its earliest stages it repudiated idolatry root and branch. Later it rejected Zoroastrian dualism. Still later it fought off the encroachments, intellectual, moral, even cultural, of the Greco-Roman world. In the Middle Ages it refused all traffic with the trinitarianism and mysteries of Christendom. And [as we shall see] there is more than one modern philosophy and ethic to which it is opposed.

Now, obviously, if Judaism were as spineless as the non-dogmatists contend, it would have lain down unhesitatingly with any and all doctrinal bedfellows. Nor could it so often and so vigorously have resisted alien ideas and values unless it had its own system of ideas and values; that is to say, a creed peculiar to itself.

The moderator speaks:

Both sides are right and both wrong, in that both have some of the truth but neither has it completely.

Judaism does in fact have a very definite religious outlook. On this point the dogmatist is quite correct.

But it is also true that Judaism has been chary about translating its outlook into precise propositions, avoiding dogmas so far as it could; and that for good and sufficient reasons.

In the first place, it requires formal creed less than do other faiths.

The Christian denominations, for example, are religious communions each of which is held together almost entirely by its special convictions. Each then needs to be very careful about defining its beliefs, or it may lose its identity.

But the Jews, as we have already observed, are not only congregants of a church, they are also members of a historic people and participants in its culture. They are Jews for other reasons than doctrine alone. Which takes some of the strain off doctrine in Judaism. Unlike Christians in their various sects, Jews can afford considerable latitude on matters of creed. Their group existence does not depend on it so immediately.

In the second place, the beginnings of Judaism were not doctrinal.

There are churches which originated in the promulgation of a set of principles drafted and published perhaps by the founders of the church, as was the case with Buddhism and Lutheranism; or by a disciple of the founder like Paul; or by some conference such as that of Nicaea which gave definitive character to the Catholic Church. Rooted in a specific declaration, these religions will tend to exhibit the exactness and articulateness of their antecedents.

Other communions, however, came into being not after the fashion of a resolution passed by a meeting but by organic growth, like a plant or person. Now, every person is a distinct entity that displays a particular personality and cherishes definite convictions. Yet he is at the same time too complex and dynamic to be caught in a network of propositions.

Brahmanism and Quakerism are religions on this order. And Judaism is, too. It has its unmistakable point of view, its own set of theses and ideals. But these are not arranged by topics, like some manifesto, all neatly ordered, with each term carefully defined and related to others. They constitute rather a climate of conviction.

Third, Judaism, to a unique degree among historic religions, has cherished and encouraged freedom of thought. Its libertarianism is in part the result of necessity. Jewish theological opinion has always ranged far and wide. Uniformity would have been unattainable had it been sought after. But even more, this tolerance of doctrinal difference expresses something basic. The Jewish religion is highly intellectualistic in the sense that it places understanding among its supreme purposes, and in the further sense that it believes in knowledge as a key to understanding. But neither knowledge nor understanding is attainable without inquiry, debate, and the right to make up one's own mind. By its nature, then, Judaism is averse to formal creeds which of necessity limit and restrain thought.

Fourth and most important, Judaism has never arrived at a creed because, highly as it rates the life of reason, it rates the good life even higher. For all its heavy intellectualism it sets morality above logic, the pursuit of justice and mercy over the possession of the correct idea. That is why the Talmud lists among those who may "acquire eternity in one instant" heathens who lack the true faith and the ignorant and simple incapable of grasping it.

And so where other historic religions have busied themselves with doctrine first and ethic second, Judaism has done just the opposite. It has concentrated its attention on giving men specific instructions on how they ought to comport themselves, especially in their dealings with one another, and left them—within limits, of course—to determine for themselves exactly how and what they should think.

Christianity speaks typically, in its essential nature, when it says: "Believe and ye shall be saved."

Judaism disposes otherwise of the issue of conviction as opposed to conduct, as can be seen in the following representative sentiment.

It is written in the book of Jeremiah: "For thus saith the Lord of hosts, the God of Israel: 'Me have they forsaken and they have not kept My law.'"

Which verse an ancient rabbi construed to mean: "Would that men forsook Me," says God, "if only they kept My law."

## 2. THE KNOWLEDGE OF GOD

"The foundation of all foundations, the pillar supporting all wisdoms, is the recognition of the reality of God."

So in the twelfth century wrote Moses Maimonides in describing the role of the God-idea in Judaism. And a most exact description it is indeed, since the Jewish religion came into being with a particular conception of God, has been committed to it ever since, and finds much of its *raison d'etre* in its advancement.

Indeed, so fundamental to Judaism is this belief that the Torah-Book simply takes it for granted, never once pausing for proof.

The opening lines of Genesis, for example, are not an argument but a declaration: "In the beginning God created the heaven and the earth."

The Decalogue does not debate, it proclaims: "I am the Lord thy God, who brought thee out of the land of Egypt, out of the house of bondage. . . ."

And it is without pausing for demonstrations, that Moses makes the climactic assertion: "Hear, O Israel: the Lord our God, the Lord is One."

Occasionally in the later books of Scripture efforts are made to adduce evidences of God's existence and nature.

"The heavens declare the glory of God," is no doubt primarily an expression of awed wonder, but there is in it also at least the suggestion of a theological inference drawn from the majesty, beauty, and orderliness of the physical world.

A clearer instance of an appeal to reason on behalf of God is to be seen in the query:

> He that planted the ear, shall He not hear?
> He that formed the eye, shall He not see?

And very often Scripture turns to the moral experiences of individuals and nations—especially of Israel—in support of its God-faith.

In classical rabbinic literature philosophical speculation is more common and thoroughgoing, though never so common as to be the norm or so thoroughgoing as to be systematic.

Not until the Middle Ages did God begin to be an object of widespread metaphysical inquiry among Jews, a Being whose existence and character are to be established by logical demonstration. But the philosophical interest, when once it appeared in Judaism, became a consuming passion, continuing vigorously for many centuries, producing a vast literature, and leaving behind as its bequest to posterity an armory of intellectual instruments for the exposition and defense of the theistic outlook.

There are arguments metaphysical:

—The argument from design, that the nature of Nature and the endowments of man are inexplicable except through God;

—The argument from causation, that an existent universe is proof presumptive of a cause at least equal to itself;

—The argument from ontology, from analyses of the structure of being.

There are arguments ethical:

—The argument from man's emotional and moral needs, that without a God to give meaning to things and sanction to ideals, human existence is pointless, aspirations are delusions, and life is devoid of purpose and hope;

—The argument from the experiences of men and nations, that only the good is stable while evil tends to destroy itself—a circumstance indicative of an ethical power as the motivating force behind the universe.

There are arguments historical based on the careers of peoples; and arguments mystical centering about the persistent reports—brought by some souls in each generation—of inner illuminations resulting from direct contact, outside thought and the senses, with Deity.

And first, last, and all the time, there are the arguments resting on revelation, prophecy, and miracle as recorded in Scripture and the Tradition.

Medieval Jewish thinkers were far from one mind on these different demonstrations. What constituted proof to one philosopher might be rejected as inconsequential by another. There were those who based almost their entire belief in God and their opinions as to His attributes on the upshot of their reasoning; and others in turn who deprecated all metaphysical inquiry as at best unnecessary, since the truth was already clear from revelation, or at worst dangerous in raising more questions than it could answer. The prevailing sentiment was that he who would speculate had the right to do so. So metaphysical inquiry came to be permanently naturalized in Judaism.

Yet even now, after centuries of Jewish philosophical research, the Torah-Book on this score as on so many others is more typical of the Jewish religion than the best metaphysical treatise. For it remains true of Judaism that it tends to assume God rather than to demonstrate Him, that it looks on Him less as a conclusion than a postulate.

Affirming God, Judaism permits considerable latitude as to conceptions of Him. It allows the individual to decide whether He is to be envisaged as transcendent or immanent, whether as an abstract principle of being as with Maimonides and the Kabbalistic mystics, or, what is more common, as supremely personal.

Not that all notions are acceptable. Judaism, as we shall see, sets standards to which God-ideas must conform if they are to pass muster. But within these there is abundant room for free play and private preference. Undogmatic generally, Judaism is undogmatic even on this point, the ground and heart of its being. Here also it is predisposed toward freedom in thought.

Indeed, here especially. For over and beyond all the factors we have already noted which have made Judaism generally libertarian on issues of theology, one more of especial potency applies here: keen awareness of the limits of man's knowledge of God.

### 3. THE LIMITS OF KNOWLEDGE

It is written in Proverbs: "In all *thy* ways know Him." Nowhere is it written: "In all *His* ways know Him."

And that for a compelling reason. Because, according to the Tradition, we cannot know God completely. At the essence of God—what He is in Himself—we can only guess; and of His manifestations or works we comprehend only that shred which our senses can grasp and our minds conceive.

That man's ignorance of God is greater than his knowledge is inscribed bold and large everywhere in the Jewish religion.

"Show me, I pray Thee, Thy glory," Moses asks of God.

"Thou canst not see My face," God responds, "for man shall not see Me and live."

In a different vein but to the same effect, the Psalmist cries out:

Such knowledge is too wonderful for me;
Too high, I cannot attain unto it. . . .
How weighty also are the thoughts of Thee unto me, O God!
How great is the sum of them!
If I would count them, they are more in number than the
    sand;
Were I to come to the end of them, I would still be with Thee.

Similarly the eleventh century neo-Platonist, Solomon ibn Gabirol, speaks of God as "the mystery in which our thoughts weary themselves to find a stay." Maimonides a century later insists that God so far transcends human comprehension that all positive descriptions of Him are inappropriate. The Kabbalists consistently characterize the Godhead as *En-Sof*, the Infinite. And an unknown medieval mystic, author of the Hebrew poem "The Hymn of Glory," epitomizes the Jewish position when he writes:

I have not seen Thee, yet I tell Thy praise,
Nor known Thee, yet I image forth Thy ways . . .

They [the prophets] told of Thee, but not as Thou must be,
Since from Thy work they tried to image Thee.

And when one reflects on the matter, it must come out
that God will forever elude us; and where He does not elude,
overwhelm us.

In the first place the God-postulate comprises all things
past, present, and future, and in addition a Being to comprehend them. On top of one infinity it places another. Little
wonder that our minds fail to contain it all.

Again, such knowledge as we have is of God's works
rather than of Him. Through the shifting veil of objects and
events we see Him as one guessed at and posited.

Finally, the physical world includes whole dominions of
whose existence we are certain but of whose quality we
have no direct experience whatsoever. But if, among the
things we know first-hand, gaps in our information yawn
so wide, what of realms less immediate to us? Must there
not be whole universes of which we have no notion at all
or at most only the faintest glimmerings? What then shall
one say about God, who embraces and transcends even these?
What else, except the trenchant words of Spinoza: that He
must possess infinite attributes in infinite degree of which
we know only a few, and these imperfectly.

Yet our ignorance of God, though stupendous and irremediable, should not be exaggerated. It is not total. If the knowledge we have of Him is not equal to our curiosity it is adequate for our needs. We know enough to have some insight
into the scheme of things and a considerable idea of how
we ought to comport ourselves.

### 4. WHAT JUDAISM SAYS ABOUT GOD

One assertion the Jewish religion makes concerning God, which, by the testimony of the Tradition itself, is the very cornerstone of Jewish theology:

*It says of God that He is one.*

This seemingly simple statement cuts deeper and runs richer than first appears. Its meanings are many and important. Of these, furthermore, each successive epoch called one or another into prominence, thus investing the single self-same affirmation with different primary significances for different generations. Yet each of these is no more than an aspect of the rounded and continuing Jewish God-faith; taken in succession they epitomize Jewish theology. On both scores they are worth reviewing.

These are the significances which history from time to time has extracted from God's oneness.

*God is one, and not many.*

The ancient world was polytheistic both as to nature and as to society.

Heathendom assumed a deity in and for each object: the river, the tree, the sun; in and for each faculty and function: fertility, memory, the artisan's skill. So it tore reality to shreds, and then, to confound confusion, assumed that each spirit had no other role except to look after its own. Under this construction there was no order, either logical or moral, to things.

In the same fashion paganism, positing a separate deity for each people, territory, and economic class, tore mankind also to shreds. For, just as a subject and his king owed political loyalty to each another and no one else, so with the relationship between a national god and his worshipers: each was expected to look out for his own exclusively, without regard for anyone else. Thus ancient religion rationalized the lawlessness of ancient society, legitimatizing the exploitation of all who stood outside the pale of protection of the local deity and lending supernatural sanctions to any attempt by the god-favored nation against its neighbors.

In proclaiming the oneness of God, therefore, the prophets intended more than a repudiation of idol worship. They were bent on establishing the principles that reality is an order, not an anarchy; that mankind is a unity, not a hodge-podge; and that one universal law of righteousness holds sway over men, transcending borders, surmounting all class lines.

At the same time and with even greater practical import their monotheism constituted a declaration of war against spiritual idolatry in all its forms: the worship to which man is addicted of the self and its desires, or of caste and group interest, or of the state and the autarch in whom it may take on symbolic embodiment. Having proclaimed the Lord alone to be God, they asserted in effect that to Him only and to His law of righteousness supremacy is to be ascribed and unreserved loyalty to be accorded.

*God is one, not two.*

Sometime in the sixth century before the Common Era, Judaism met Zoroastrianism, encountering for the first time a religion rivaling itself in maturity, spirituality, and earnestness. Distinctive of this faith was its doctrine of dualism. Behind the world it discerned not one but two creative beings, the first a force of light and goodness, the other a power of darkness and evil. These twin genii wrestle ceaselessly for the world and man's soul, a struggle in which each human being, willy-nilly, takes sides. Religion's purpose, as Zoroastrianism conceived it, is to make certain that men choose the right side.

This theology has its attractions. It is dramatic in its picture of a world conflict, heroic in the demands it makes of man, and metaphysically alluring, since it offers—or seems to offer—a quick solution to the enigma of evil.

Despite all this, Judaism rejected it. Whatever its advantages, the disabilities of dualism proved greater.

Dualism makes an absolute of evil; Judaism regards evil as contingent to a prior and more basic good.

Dualism despairs in advance of half of reality and half of human nature. Judaism holds that there is nothing which cannot be retrieved for the good. The most sinful impulses in man, as the rabbis point out, are the very forces which, properly directed, motivate the virtues.

Dualism places the ultimate triumph of the good in jeopardy. If the dark be correlative to the light, what assurance is there that the latter will prevail?

Judaism's repudiation of Zoroastrianism was not achieved in a moment. For centuries the possibility of "two powers" continued to tempt the Jewish imagination. But the first reaction of the prophet when he insisted that one and the same God "fashions light and creates darkness, makes peace and creates evil,"—that remained in the end the Tradition's last word. *

* For the philosopher, dualism is negated by the additional consideration that it raises a riddle greater than any it solves: the question of the relation between its two first principles. Indeed, the very phrase "two first principles" is a contradiction in terms. Now, if a prime purpose of metaphysical speculation is to account for the universe, dualism fails to pass the first test of any acceptable cosmology.

*God is one, not three.*

During the Middle Ages the Jewish assertion of God's unity became an explicit denial of the Christian dogma of the Trinity, a total disavowal of the thesis that God, though one, is somehow at the same time three persons, "coeternal and coequal."

In rejecting this doctrine Jews were concerned primarily with warding off what they regarded as a misrepresentation of the Divine nature. But they were no less zealous to indicate their dissent from the notion, integral to the Trinity, of a God-man: Deity embodied in the flesh and blood of some particular individual. To them all men reflect God's nature and are His children. The suggestion that any single human being might be God Himself they spurned as blasphemy.

*God is one, not none.*

So in our day Judaism declares its unyielding opposition to contemporary atheism and the materialism that attends it; to the new, yet old, misreading of reality as the blind interplay of matter and energy; to the error that man and his values are children of cosmic chance, destined to perish as pointlessly as they came to be.

So also the Tradition protests against another and scarcely less dangerous modern fallacy, the evasive proposition that God *is* but does not *exist,* that He is only a human conception or a useful fiction, or that His name may properly be assigned to the highest value a man cherishes. Against all such slippery counsels Judaism affirms that God's existence is independent of man and that He is not only actual and real but the most actual actuality and realest reality of all.

In the end then, the Tradition at the latest stage in its career takes its stand again on the same verity which first gave it life and character.

## 5. OTHER ATTRIBUTES OF GOD

Judaism says further concerning God:

—That He is the *Creator* of all things through all time. Nor is His creativity to be viewed as a lone episode in the past, a tossing out, as it were, of the cosmic ball which is then allowed to roll where it will. On the contrary, He continues to sustain and animate the universe, ever evoking new things and regenerating the old, even as the prayerbook asserts: "He reneweth in His goodness, every day continually, the work of Creation."

—That He is *Spirit*, which is to say, that He is at one and the same time a Mind that contemplates and a Power at work. To put it in different words, that He is Reason and Purpose.

It is in this respect that man, instinct with thought and will, is closest akin to God. Wherefore the medieval philosopher-poet, Solomon ibn Gabirol, enumerating the "three things which stand together to bring the awareness of Thee ever before me," lists first the heavens and second the earth in its expanse, but as a climactic third "the stirring of my heart when I look inward."

—That He is *Lawgiver*, and that in three senses.

He is the source not only of the natural law to which the physical world conforms but also of the moral law regulative of human existence.

He is the mind disclosed in revelation.

He is the guarantor of morality, the rectifier of disturbed
balances, and the power that enforces the right.

—That He is the *Guide of History*.

To Judaism history is the unfolding of a design of which
the dénouement is to be man's ultimate fulfillment and redemption.

Behind this drama stands God: playwright, director, ani-
mator, spectator, critic, and—from within every character
and setting—actor also. Wherefore the Tradition speaks frequently of Him as the God of the Patriarchs, of the Exodus,
and of Sinai; that is, of the past; or in terms of His Kingdom
to come, of the future; in sum, as the God of the cosmic and
the human adventure.

—That He is man's *Helper*.

God's assistance to man is not to be espied only or even
primarily in spectacular and crucial incidents. It is much
more a matter of what the traditional prayerbook describes
as "Thy miracles which are daily with us, Thy wonders
and goodnesses which are wrought at all times, evening,
morn, and noon"; that is to say, of the normalities of human
experience.

Thus God is forever helping man through the resources
and dependability of the physical world.

He helps man further through man's own body, skilled,
adaptable, resilient; through his mind, eager and ingenious;
through his heart, life-loving, courageous, and aspiring.

He helps man through the medium of other men; their
capacity for cooperation; the social wealth and technical
informations they have amassed together; the love and understanding they afford one another; the political devices
and civil liberties which protect them in life and freedom;

their sciences, arts, religions, all the cultural treasures accumulated throughout the ages and handed on as patrimony to each new generation; through, in sum, all the institutions, practices, and assistances which are rendered by individuals to one another and by society to all its members.

He helps man by the very thought of Himself, a clarifying, meaning-giving, hope-inspiring thought.

(Does He help man by miracles, too; by intervening in the course of Nature, breaching its laws for human ends? To this question almost all traditionalists answer _Yes_, almost all modernists _No_.)

And, as the Tradition teaches and almost all professing Jews believe, He helps men from Himself by the inflow of His spirit into their hearts, either in response to prayer or through mystical communion or in the course of the normal respiration of the soul. Invading them, He renders them strong with a strength they did not possess heretofore, sharp-sighted with an unusual insight, and compassionate with a mercy they have not otherwise known.

—That He is the _Liberator_ of men and their societies.

God is the Power working within individuals and peoples that will not permit them to acquiesce in servitude, their own or that of others. He is the spark that kindles them into rebellion and the iron that makes them stubborn for freedom's sake. And simultaneously He hardens the heart of tyrants, until lost to reason, incapable of either learning or forgetting, they destroy themselves.

Of God's emancipations all peoples have had experience, but Israel especially, most particularly when it was brought forth from Egypt by a mighty hand and an outstretched arm. Wherefore the Exodus is to Jews, as indeed to much of mankind, the classic instance of liberation; a proof that, since God *is*, every bondage, political, economic, or spiritual, can be and someday will be broken.

—That He is the *Savior* of souls.

Men may be enslaved not only from without but by inner blindness, weakness, and perversity. External deliverance therefore does not suffice; there is need of salvation also.

Salvation, as the Tradition construes it, may pertain to life-after-death; its primary reference, however, from the Jewish viewpoint, is to this world.

Salvation is man's victory over his limitations: ignorance, for instance, or insensitivity; it is his conquest of sinfulness, of the evils resident within him, such as pride, selfishness, hate, lust, cynicism, the deliberate rejection of goodness and truth.

Against these and other perversions, God stands as Savior. The very awareness of Him is a saving power, helping to emancipate the human spirit from the restraints that frustrate it, from the wickednesses that corrupt it from within. All the more, He Himself, now driving man relentlessly by *force majeure*, now leading him gently—even guilefully— but ever and constantly moving him to the redemption of his soul.

## 6. ENVISAGEMENTS

Such are the classic attributes of God as the Tradition propounds them.

The range of freedom they allow is considerable.

Each of them is elastic, amenable to diverse interpretations. They may be differently arranged. And every person makes his own selection of which to stress and elaborate, which to pass over lightly or leave bare.

Thus it comes to pass that, proceeding from shared elements, each soul arrives at a very personal envisagement of God.

The naive understand Him according to their simplicity, the sophisticated according to their subtlety.

Rationalists comprehend Him through reason, mystics by intuition, traditionalists in Torah, moralists via the good life.

Some interpret and modify old conceptions of Him in the light of contemporary science and philosophy; others retain them both in form and content as they have come down from the past.

So in the end each man makes of the common God of Judaism his own God, an envisagement unique and peculiar to him, something intimate and private and therefore warm and compelling.

Along with and as part of this individualizing of God goes a pictorializing of Him.

If the metaphysically minded among theologians are to be believed, this process is far from laudable. God, Maimonides argued, is not a body and bears no resemblance to a body; and no analogies to Him from the corporeal may properly be drawn.

But drawn they are nonetheless, and not only by common folk but even by the metaphysicians who frown on them.

The truth is that the pictorialization of abstract ideas is unavoidable. This is the way the mind functions: with images gross or delicate.

As a matter of fact, despite purists like Maimonides, the Tradition as a whole has seen nothing illegitimate or dangerous in parables of Deity, so long as, by a paradox which is really no paradox, they are recognized as illegitimate and dangerous, and in consequence are carefully measured out and then taken with a grain of salt.

Now the possible analogies of God are innumerable. Jewish religious literature is replete with them, in bewildering variety.

But through their profusion two major patterns show.

The first emphasizes the apartness of God from the world, His otherness; the second, His nearness and in-ness.

Of the former class, a fair sampling may be taken from a medieval hymn of unknown authorship, recited to this day in traditionalist synagogues on the eve of the Day of Atonement.

In the successive stanzas this poem describes the relation of man and the world to God as that of the clay to the potter, the stone to the mason, the iron to the smith, the anchor to the pilot, the glass to the blower, the tapestry to the embroiderer, the silver to the refiner and, in a return to the first figure, which is also the most satisfactory, of the clay to the potter.

All these envisagements are acceptable on some grounds and quite as unacceptable on others.

They are acceptable in that they portray the world for what in the religious view it is in fact: the simultaneous object of the thought and action of God.

Except that—and here is the catch in images of this order —the potter neither creates his clay nor inhabits it nor constitutes the ground of its existence. God is not so separate from the world as the parable suggests.

Wherefore one is driven to the second type of parable, that which underscores God's immanence.

In these too the Tradition is well dowered. There are the old Talmudic envisagements of the Divine as the *Shechinah* or near Presence; and the Kabbalistic and Hasidic pictorializations of Him as the Seed to which physical reality is the pod, or the Spark from which the flame of the universe outflares.

The classic allegory along these lines is that in which God is spoken of as the Soul of the world, an analogue well worked through in the following homily from rabbinic literature:

It is written in Psalms, "Bless the Lord, O my soul."

Why did David bid his soul in particular to praise God? Because he said, "As the soul pervades the body, God pervades the world. . . . As the soul sustains the body, God sustains the world. . . . As the soul survives the body, God survives the world. . . . As there is a unitary and single soul in the body, so there is but a unitary and single God to the world. . . . Wherefore let the soul of the body praise Him who is, as it were, the soul of the world."

Quite clearly this parable of the divine nature is more adequate in some respects than those first considered. This time God is no longer presented as removed from the universe but as within it: its unifying, animating principle.

Yet this image, too, does not stand up under examination. For, though we strain to avoid it, we cannot help thinking of soul and body as somehow coextensive and mutually determinative. God however transcends the universe and is independent of it.

One envisagement, and one envisagement only, comes really close to catching the simultaneous immanence and transcendence of God. That is the figure, so frequently encountered in Jewish religious literature, of God as Father. A father is on the one side distinct from his child. And yet, because he has bestowed being and character on him, he is also in him.

But even this metaphor, while better than the others and possessing the additional advantage of bespeaking love and compassion, suffers the disability of being heavily anthropomorphic.

There is then, let us admit it at last, no adequate description of God. Being human, we cannot resist the impulse to pictures. But none of our allegories can be the full truth, or for that matter any more than a dark and garbled hint.

God, to put it baldly, is too big for us. Our similes and tropes are to Him as buckets to an ocean. Each may carry a little of His character; none of them and not all of them together can hold His entirety.

Or, as the medieval mystic sang in the *Hymn of Glory:*

> Men have parabled of Thee in many figures;
> Lo, through all their images, Thou art one.

## 7. THE GREAT SHADOW

Across the light of God evil throws a shadow.

If He *is*, why is the world not better? Why is it so marred and weighted down with disorder and suffering that it seems at times not the handiwork of a God of goodness but the contrivance of a fiend?

These terrible questions are as old in Judaism as the God-faith itself. Nor does the Tradition have a single response for them. It offers instead all the answers framed by all who ever wrestled with the problem. And since no generation and no individual has ever been spared the painful necessity of justifying God's ways, the answers are many and varied indeed.

These are they, grouped into logical classes:

I. There are the theories which seek to account for evil in moral terms; among them the following:

That an evil may be the result of some prior sin of the individual on whom it is visited; that it is often punitive even where it seems not to be, since the antecedent sin may have escaped notice or may go unassociated with its consequence.

That it may represent the expiation of the wrong-doing not of an individual but of his community; that if a man avails himself of the advantages afforded him by his society, he must be prepared to take responsibility for its iniquities.

That it is necessary so that man may be a moral being. For how, if there were no evil, could man choose the good?

That it must be or the good would also not exist, or else, if it existed, would pass unrecognized for want of contrast.

That it is indispensable to man's character, since, were it not for its prodding, no one would ever bestir himself, let alone develop attachments to justice, compassion, and love.

That it supplies men with a touchstone on which they may test the stuff of which they are made, an adversary against whom to contend and so grow strong; a contest without which there could be no victory.

II. There are the theories which seek to account for evil in metaphysical terms; among them the following:

That evil has no reality in itself but is merely the absence of good.

That it appears as evil because it is seen isolated or in a partial view.

That what men call evils are only instances of the laws of life which happen to strike them adversely. If they are prepared to accept the benefits of these rules, what valid complaint have they when these same rules work to their disadvantage?

III. There are the theories which seek to account for evil as something temporary and destined in the end to be transcended and retrieved; among them the following:

That it will be compensated and made good in life after death, and here on earth in God's Kingdom to come.

That it represents the survival into the human condition of other, lower stages of reality, mineral, vegetable, and animal, out of which man has emerged, or on which he stands; that the traces of these are being erased with time and the further unfolding of God's purpose until some day man will be perfectly and purely human.

IV. There is, finally, the theory that evil is inscrutable, an enigma beyond unraveling, to which the answer, if any, is known to God alone. This is the moral of the ending of the Book of Job where Job lays his hand on his lips in contrition and confession of ignorance. This is the purport of the rabbinic epigram: "It is not in our power to explain either the tranquillity of the wicked or the sufferings of the upright."

Here, no more than listed, are some of the many suggestions advanced by Judaism on the theme of evil. Among these the individual Jew is free to make his selection, adopting the response or combination of responses which best satisfies him.

At which one is impelled to inquire: "Is that the best the Tradition can do with the most desperate *impasse* of the human spirit? Has it no better counsel than to say 'Here are some notions which have at various times been current in Judaism. Help yourself. Take one; take none; take all; take some'?"

The criticism, though it seems fair enough at first, turns out on reflection to be quite unreasonable. We are looking, let us remember, for an acceptable theodicy; that is to say, for such an explanation of evil as will reconcile the fact of it with the existence of God. But quite obviously no theodicy can be a cover-all, big and adaptable enough to be spread over any and all theologies. To the contrary, each must be relative to some particular God-idea. But Judaism, promulgating no single authoritative envisagement of God, very naturally has no single official theodicy to propound.

More decisively, the Jewish religion, as already noted, has always been disposed to give men their choice among opinions if only they behaved as was right.

Dealing with evil, Judaism runs true to character. It makes no effort to attain conformity on points of theory, but it is crisp and clear on what it expects by way of behavior.

It expects a man, no matter what else he may think about evil, to recognize it as something to be fought and to go out and fight it.

It expects that he will care for its victims, comforting the mourners, feeding the hungry, clothing the naked, healing the sick, enlightening the ignorant, defending the oppressed, liberating the enslaved.

It expects him to root out its causes from the world of nature, from his own soul, and from society.

And as for the uncorrectible evils of the human lot, those which cannot be fought off or remedied by any means whatsoever, Judaism expects him to endure these with dignity and courage, mitigating their bitterness and hurt with the medicaments of faith, utilizing them to the purification and refinement of his soul.

Throughout, it is almost as though Judaism were saying to men, "By all means strive after insight into this mystery, and may God's favor attend your quest; but never permit yourselves to forget that a *practical* approach to the problem is always before you; that you have it in your power to eliminate many, perhaps most, of the ills that afflict men."

One other expectation Judaism entertains as to its communicants: it assumes that they will keep their heads religiously, refusing to be demoralized by evil, no matter how large and grim.

The God-faith rests on solid grounds, grounds that would be sufficient even were men altogether impotent before the world's badness.

Wherefore it devolves on every spiritually responsible person to stand by the integrity of his faith.

Or, as was said long ago by a man well acquainted with sorrow:

"Though He slay me, yet will I trust in Him."

## 8. BETWEEN GOD AND MAN

Between God and man stands no one—not God-man, not angel, not advocate. Nor is intercession or intervention required.

As nothing comes between soul and body, father and child, potter and vessel, so nothing separates man from God, Soul of his soul, his Father and Fashioner.

To be sure, out of their obtuseness or bewilderment men may fail to perceive how close He is to them. Through their sins they may make themselves unworthy of His presence and come to feel alienated from Him. But no one can push Him away or estrange Him altogether. And if a need arise for a rediscovery of God or a return to Him, then each man must accomplish this on his own account. Is he blind? He must learn to see for himself, since no one can see on his behalf. Is he lost? He must find his own way home.

Other men may help him. They may give him courage, guidance, instruction; they may blaze trails and set examples. But in the end, sight is not sight if it is vicarious. Companionship, whether with God or anyone else, must be immediate or it is not companionship.

In sum, there is and can be no vicarious salvation. Each man must redeem his own soul.

# THE GOOD LIFE

V

## 1. THE GOODNESS OF LIFE

"And God saw everything that He had made, and, behold, it was very good."

So with almost its first words Scripture states a thesis that echoes and re-echoes down the centuries and throughout the Tradition:

Life is good.

Wherefore a man should treasure it, not despise it; affirm and not deny it; have faith in it and never despair of its possibilities. For behind it is God.

Life is good and man can find it such, provided—and this is the great condition to everything else—that it is properly lived.

Even as it is written, "See, I have set before thee this day life and good, and death and evil, in that I command thee this day to love the Lord thy God, to walk in His ways, and to keep His commandments and His statutes and His ordinances . . . therefore choose life, that thou mayest live, thou and thy seed."

## 2. MAN——AND HIS WILL

What is man?

A creature of dust; a thing of transience whose days fly

by faster than a weaver's shuttle; a fragile being, crushed sooner than a moth; a body, sustaining and reproducing itself after the fashion of the beasts; a vessel filled with shame and confusion, impelled by pride and self-love, driven by passions.

All these, says the Tradition, is man.

But he is also more and other.

The handiwork, the child, the mirrored image of God, fashioned after and instinct with Him, he displays, though in infinitely lesser degree and with innumerable flaws, the powers ascribed to and associated with Divinity: the ability to think and create, the awareness of the good and beautiful, the capacity for love and compassion, and freedom of the will.

Wherefore, concerning him who is simultaneously near-God and near-brute, the Psalmist cries out in almost one and the same breath:

"What is man that Thou art mindful of him? . . . Yet Thou hast made him but little lower than the angels."

Man's freedom of will is far from absolute, as the Tradition concedes readily and as the most elemental experience confirms.

Since we have bodies, we are subject to the conditions of all things corporeal. We cannot, no matter how we desire it, be in two places at once, nor live at any other time than that in which we find ourselves. We may be limited further, sometimes to the point of impotence, by deficiencies in our physical or mental equipment, by conditions imposed by birth, or by large-scale social forces amove in our time. Numerous and strong are the circumscriptions, possible and actual, on our liberty. But within them some open space always remains.

This is the arena of moral decision. It may be cramped and narrow, often little more than a succession of slits and interstices in the tissue of circumstance, predetermined and determining. But it is large enough for man's size, and broad enough for him to show his mettle. The direction he takes, how far he goes along it, how hard he tries to move (even when he fails to budge an inch), suffice to establish his quality and worth.

This is the point of a bold, penetrating aphorism struck off by the third century Palestinian rabbi, Hanina ben Pappa, who held that before a human being is conceived in his mother's womb God has already ordained concerning him "whether he shall be strong or weak, intelligent or dull, rich or poor. But whether he shall be wicked or virtuous is not pronounced. Nor can even God predetermine this, since [as was taught by another and somewhat earlier Rabbi Hanina] 'all things are in Heaven's hands except man's reverence for Heaven.'"

### 3. THE NATURE OF THE GOOD

To know good and evil, says Genesis, is to be like God. Certainly it is to be as distinctively and essentially human as is possible to man.

But what is the good? In what does it consist?

As we experience it, it is ten times ten thousand diverse actions, responses, moods, thoughts, desires, hopes, most of them seemingly irrelevant to one another. Is the good then no more than a word, a catch-all for anything and everything of which anybody happens to approve? Or does it have a character of its own? Is there among the instances of it some common denominator?

On these points Judaism is as exact and exacting as it is accommodating on theology. Goodness, it insists, is more than a name; it is a quality objectively present in men and their conduct. (It may also inhere in objects, forces, and circumstances in so far as they bear on moral values.) To denote and describe this quality the Jewish religion uses a variety of phrases. Their number should not mislead us. They all stand for either the same actuality or different aspects of it.

This is the good, according to the formulas of the Tradition:

—*To do the will of God;* that is, for men to obey His moral law as things physical conform to the laws of nature.

—*To reveal His glory;* that is, for men to elicit such nobility from themselves and others and society as to unveil the divinity resident in all things, causing mankind to marvel as did Jacob of old: "Surely the Lord is in this place; and I knew it not."

Conversely it is of the nature of evil-doing that, in the terminology of Jewish mysticism, it shall "banish the Presence from the world," or "diminish the stature of Deity"; that is to say, make it hard for men to perceive God and believe in Him.

—*To hallow His name;* that is, to invest life so richly with dignity and beauty that glory redounds to Him who animates it. Every righteous or kindly deed has this effect; every such deed therefore is said by the Tradition to constitute a "hallowing of the Name." Applicable as this concept is to even the most commonplace of human actions, it pertains especially to instances of heroism and self-negation on behalf of love, justice, and truth. Indeed, the standard Hebrew phrase for martyrdom is none other than *Kiddush Hashem* "sanctification of the Name"; for in man's sacrifice of life on behalf of a valid ideal, God is hallowed supremely.

—*To imitate Him;* that is, for the human soul to accent its origin in and kinship with God by exhibiting godly traits.

This is the significance of the saying of Scripture: "After the Lord your God shall ye walk . . . and unto Him shall ye cleave."

This too is the purport of the exhortation of an ancient sage: "Let us make ourselves like Him. As He is merciful and gracious, so let us strive to be."

—*To advance God's Kingdom;* that is, to cooperate with Him as He drives toward the fullness of freedom, truth, and goodness in men and human affairs.

Or to commute all these formulas into the master canon of Jewish morality:

*The good for man is to perform the* MIZVOTH, *the commandments of the Torah.* For he who does this does all else also; he obeys the will of God, reveals His glory, hallows His name, imitates Him, and hastens the advent of His Kingdom on earth.

### 4. BETWEEN MAN AND GOD

To do the commandments . . .

And the first of these is the love of God.

First in enumeration, since the Ten Commandments begin with the declaration: "I am the Lord thy God. . . ."

First logically, for from it the rest of Jewish morality can be deduced.

First genetically, in the sense that out of this, much of Judaism unfolded.

Nor is the love of God a strange or esoteric virtue, something too hard or exalted for an ordinary man. To the contrary it is, as Moses attested, "very nigh unto thee, in thy mouth, and in thy heart, that thou mayest do it."

Except in magnitude and gravity it would seem to resemble man's love for anything which is not physical or in which the physical is an irrelevancy. Any such "platonic" love consists in an intense awareness of another, an appreciation of its nature, gratitude for its presence, the urge to understand it, to be at peace with it, to serve its purposes, to make it and its excellences known, to build one's life upon it.

Substitute the word "God" for "another" and "His" for "its" in the preceding paragraph, invest the whole with the grandeur and passion proper to so immense an object, and something akin to the love of God unfolds.

The fear of God, the counterpoise to the love of Him, is compounded of many ingredients: awe of infinite greatness; recoil before an ineffable mystery; the conviction, born through contrast, of man's fragility.

Present in it, too, is a triple dread:

—The dread which the clay on the potter's wheel might feel over the weird shapes and terrible destinies into which it may be fashioned;

—The dread of the lawbreaker before the judge;

—The dread of the engineer who knows that ruin may await him and his works should he deviate even by a hair's breadth from the principles of his science.

There are in all communions some individuals who are made unhappy by any reference to the fear of God. They are sentimentalists, wishful thinkers, or cowards—persons either ignorant of the nature of things or too timid to face them. No one who sees reality as it is, bitter as well as sweet, violent as well as gentle, frightening as well as comforting, will question for a moment that God is as fittingly an object of dread as of love.

Yet, between the two, says the Tradition, love ought to be the stronger, such a love as that of which Rabbi Akiba taught when he said: "It is written in Scripture, 'Thou shalt love the Lord thy God . . . with all thy soul.'"

"Which means," Rabbi Akiba expounded, "even at the moment when He taketh away thy soul."

(And having spoken so, he went off to practice his preachment in martyrdom.)

On this intuition of the supremacy of love Judaism stands when it prescribes that the dying shall proclaim as their last words: "Hear, O Israel, the Lord our God, the Lord is One."

This conviction inspires the *Kaddish* prayer, assigned in the Tradition for recitation by those newly bereaved: "Magnified and sanctified be His great name, in the world which He has created according to His will, and may He establish His Kingdom. . . ."

So, bowed by the last mystery and fiercest ordeal of human experience, the soul lifts itself up to reaffirm life and God.

In which the love of God attains its climax and triumph.

### 5. THE DUTIES OF THE HEART

It is with himself that a man lives always and most intimately. Hence he requires urgently an acquaintance with those principles which bear on his private existence, the precepts which Bahya ibn Pakuda, moralist of the eleventh century, called "the duties of the heart."

Of these one has already been listed: the interwoven love and fear of God described in the preceding chapter.

Next after this comes the obligation to understanding. And a prime obligation it is, since a man must know what is proper in order to think, feel, and act as he ought. Wherefore the ancient rabbis used to say, "An ignorant man cannot be truly devout."

The life of reason is necessary further as a means whereby men may reveal the Divinity lodged in them. Is not God reason? Can kinship with Him be better asserted or His nature more effectively imitated than in the cultivation of the truth?

Thus, when Moses Maimonides asserted that the climax of the religious life and the perfection of man consists in "the possession of the highest intellectual faculties and of such notions as lead to true metaphysical opinions," he was speaking in large part as an Aristotelian, but in no slight measure as a Jew, as was the case centuries later with Spinoza also and his ideal of the *amor intellectualis dei.*

The main stream of the Tradition does not go so far. In its eyes moral excellence stands higher than intellectual, the merciful and just heart above the head no matter how informed and discerning. But if not at the apex of its triangle of values, understanding is not much below it. And while the heroes of Judaism are good men before they are wise, they are usually wise as well as good.

Wisdom and learning are not the same thing. Many a man innocent of all book knowledge has distilled from experience and reflection the fundamentals of human existence. And many a man has studied much and remained a fool. For such persons rabbinic literature has a special, barbed phrase: "Asses laden with books."

But though learning is not indispensable to wisdom it is normally a first and long step in its direction. Very naturally and wisely the Tradition asks of its faithful that they acquire knowledge, knowledge as to itself in the first instance, but general learning as well.

To Judaism uniquely among religions the processes of learning are sacred and study a holy pursuit. Nor has any other communion thought through and worked out as thoroughly the morality appropriate to scholarship.

Here are some passages on this theme taken at random from the Tradition.

On the disciplines of study:

"The bashful learneth not, the impatient teacheth not."

"Set a fixed time for study."

"This is the way of the study of Torah: a morsel of bread with salt shalt thou eat, water meted out shalt thou drink, on the ground shalt thou sleep, a life of travail shalt thou lead while thou toilest in the Torah. But if thou doest so, happy art thou and it is well with thee."

On the occupational hazard of bookmen, pride in knowledge:

"As wine keepeth not in vessels of silver and gold but only in earthenware, so learning remaineth wholesome only in the humble."

"Why is Torah compared to water? To teach thee that as water floweth away from the lofty and gathereth only in lowly places, so with wisdom among men."

On the dignity of knowledge:

"Better the lowest born who is a scholar, than a high priest who is an ignoramus."

On the danger of self-deception:

"Let a man revere God as much in secret as in public, ever acknowledge the truth, and speak the truth in his own heart."

On the joys of reading, the counsel of a medieval savant:

"My son! Make thy books thy companions, let thy cases and shelves be thy pleasure grounds and gardens. Bask in their paradise, gather their fruit, pluck their roses, take their spices and myrrh. If thy soul be satiate and weary, move from garden to garden, from flower bed to flower bed, from one view to another. Then will thy desire renew itself, and thy soul be filled with delight."

From the last testament of still another medieval Jew:

"Each [of my children] shall always have in his house a desk on which one or two volumes of the Talmud shall rest, or some similar work, so that on entering his home he may be tempted to open a book."

And finally, on the obligation to stand by the truth as one sees it against, if need be, Almighty God Himself, the following revealing legend from the Talmud:

Tradition has it that on that day Rabbi Eliezer advanced every conceivable argument without persuading his fellows.

Whereupon he said to them, "If the law be according to my opinion, then let yon carob tree prove it." And a carob tree moved one hundred cubits from its place!

To which they responded, "What sort of demonstration does a carob tree afford?"

Whereupon he said to them a second time, "If the law be according to my opinion, let yon stream prove it." And the stream flowed backward!

To which they responded, "What sort of demonstration does a stream afford?"

Whereupon he said to them, "If the law be according to my opinion, let the walls of this academy prove it."

And the walls bent to the point of falling until Rabbi Joshua rebuked them saying, "When scholars contend with one another, what business have ye among them?"

And so they did not fall out of respect for Rabbi Joshua, and they did not straighten out of respect for Rabbi Eliezer but remain slanting to this day.

Whereupon Rabbi Eliezer persisted and said to them, "If the law be according to my opinion, let them prove it from on high."

And a heavenly voice sounded forth and said, "What have ye against Rabbi Eliezer after whose opinion the law is always to be framed?"

At which Rabbi Joshua arose and said, "The Torah declares concerning itself, 'It is not up in heaven'; that is to say, once the Torah was given on Mount Sinai, we pay no heed to heavenly voices but, as the Torah ordains further, we follow the opinion of the majority."

Through which tale it becomes clear that the magnificent impudence of Job was no freak in Judaism, that as he advocated the requirements of conscience against God Himself, so the Jewish religion expects its faithful to defend reason not only against men and human error but, if such a contingency can be imagined, against the very hosts of Heaven.

### 6. GRANDEUR AND LOWLINESS

To be human is to *know*. And among the things a man can know perhaps the most wonderful is that he is human. "Precious is man," said Rabbi Akiba, "since he is created in God's image. But especial is the grace whereby it is known to him that he is created in God's image."

From the presence in man of a divine element two implications flow:

He owes himself self-respect, a dignity of thought and action befitting one in whom burns a spark of God.

And he is under the duty to express his individuality. For bearing the divine image, he bears it uniquely. No one in all the world exactly duplicates him. Therefore he is obliged to discover and develop his uniqueness. Otherwise, to all eternity some aspect of the divine nature shall have been left latent and unfulfilled.

The duties of the heart, so far enumerated, are all conducive to an exalted opinion of man. But such an appraisal may, given the least exaggeration, become arrogance. Wherefore the Tradition is careful to include in private morality the commandment to humility.

Man may be the crown of creation, but he is totally a creature. God, not he, made him, his faculties, his world. What is more, he serves the good, if at all, in no more than infinitesimal degree, and then with many an interval of truancy and unfaithfulness.

Let him then be congruously modest, as mindful of his lowliness as of his grandeur. Let the consciousness that he is little less than an angel be offset by the awareness that he is little higher than a beast. Let him, in a word, be humble. For what is humility but this: the balance and proportion whereby one sees himself for no more or better than he is in fact?

### 7. BODY AND SOUL

The tension between body and soul which so harrowed first the pagan world and then the Christian is relaxed in Judaism. To the age-old question: which shall a man gratify, his flesh or his spirit, Judaism answers simply, "both."

But what of conflicts between the two? What about the times, and these not infrequent, when impulse turns one way and conscience another, when between "want" and "ought" we are all but torn asunder?

From this spiritual predicament men have in the main taken one of two exits: they have given in to the body, forgetting the soul; or deferred to the soul, suppressing the body. Neither course has served them particularly well.

Sensuality has rarely made men happy and often left them sick. This has been so whether the indulgence was reckless and gross after the pattern of the Sybarites of all ages, or prudent as recommended by Epicurus, or refined and exquisite as urged by Walter Pater.

The other tactic is asceticism, best represented in ancient paganism by Plato and Plotinus, and thanks to Paul of Tarsus a permanent element in historic Christianity. From this viewpoint, the flesh and its desires are evil, conducive only to ensnaring the soul in things carnal, amid which it is first corrupted and then destroyed, according to the saying of the old Greek mystics: *soma sema esti*, "the body is a tomb." Wherefore man has no alternative except to deny the flesh.

Unfortunately this theory has functioned no better than its alternative.

In the first place it is impracticable. The body will not be suppressed. The attempt to coerce it involves so much self-policing that little energy is left for other occupations of the spirit.

Then, too, this course leads to self-contradiction. Universalized and pushed to its logical consequence, it would spell death for the individual and dissolution for society.

Finally, asceticism has encouraged pruriency, spurious innocence. Its influence on marriage and the love relationship has been especially unfortunate. Having degraded the sex impulse, it has caused many a man to despise himself for his desires and to be ashamed of their gratification. By presenting marriage as a concession to human weakness, it has turned into a second-best what is, properly regarded, the loveliest and most ennobling of all human associations.

Judaism has avoided both errors, the sensualist and the ascetic.

Thus, the Tradition has no sympathy with the unprincipled indulgence of desire. Indeed, so intensely did the ancient rabbis disapprove of it that they converted the word "Epicurean" into an epithet for the man capable of every impiety and crime.

But if Judaism will have no traffic with sensualism in one direction, it turns away from asceticism in the other. In its view, the body, no less the work of God than the soul, cannot be inherently evil. Self-negation is not necessarily virtuous. On the contrary, it may be thoroughly sinful, either by offending against physical health and mental stability, or by rendering happiness inaccessible. For, the Tradition insists, it is man's obligation to enjoy life; part of religion's function is to help him do so. Pleasure then must be not only legitimate but mandatory.

Wherefore Scripture ordains, "Thou shalt rejoice before the Lord, thy God," which the rabbis interpret to include not only joys of the spirit such as worship, study, and good works but those of the body also, "food and drink, raiment and fellowship."

Similarly, according to the judgment of an ancient sage: "He who sees a legitimate pleasure and does not avail himself of it is an ingrate against God who made it possible."

All in all, historic Judaism, though it has often manifested ascetic tendencies, has never accepted them as normal.

But what of the evil appetites in human nature, the self-love, pride, and lust?

They are there, of course; and the Tradition has much to say about their origins, nature and how they may be mastered. But few of them are irremediably evil; each of them under some favoring circumstance subserves the good. As Rabbi Nahman ben Samuel observed so shrewdly: "Were it not for the 'evil impulse' no man would ever build a house, take a wife, beget a child, or engage in business."

Even selfishness, the most dangerous of human traits, has its proper place. A modicum of it is a *sine qua non*. "If I am not for myself, who will be for me?" asked Hillel, going on, however, to add, "If I am for myself alone, what do I amount to?"

Competitiveness too, for all the ills good. Witness the saying: "The rivalry wisdom."

All depends, with the passions, on the controls to which they are subjected and the ends to which they are turned.

At which point Judaism's special contribution to the problem emerges.

The Tradition holds that a man should seek neither to thwart his body altogether nor to glut it, but to sanctify it. By which is meant:

—First, that he shall accept upon himself the ethical principles laid down by the Torah: its "yoke," as the Tradition names it. Having so subordinated himself to a moral code, he shall then allow it to decide between flesh and spirit, permitting himself whatever it sanctions, foregoing what it forbids.

—Second, that he shall invest everything he does, no matter how menial or carnal, with *Kedushah*, or holiness; that is to say, with intimations of the divine and ideal.

It is right and good that he shall eat with relish. But let his meal be more than the appeasing of hunger. Let it serve as an occasion for the strengthening of family ties, for the association of friends, for the exchange of "words of Torah and wisdom." Let it be hallowed further with religious exercises. So a man may eat ever so zestfully and still be no beast. His table is an altar.

Sex, too, is sanctified in the wedlock marked by love. Nor is marriage commended merely on the sorry theory that it is to be preferred to burning. On the contrary, the Tradition looks on the love relationship as a high adventure of the human spirit; an opportunity for a man and woman to make a oneness of their separateness, confirm each other in strength and support each other in weakness, be schooled in unselfishness and compassion, and help to hand on from their generation to the next the sacred things of their community.

On all these scores, Judaism holds it to be man's duty to marry and rear children. Conversely, it views voluntary abstinence from marriage as a triple sin—against the health of body, the fulfillment of soul, and the welfare of society.

On which thesis the ancient rabbis contrived one of their most ingenious bits of word play:

The Hebrew word *Iish,* meaning "man," contains a letter "i" which is missing from the word *Ishah* "woman"; just as *Ishah* has in it an "h" lacking in *Iish.*

Now these two letters "i" and "h" when joined together spell out a Hebrew name for God. On the other hand, when they are deleted from *Iish* and *Ishah* respectively what remains in either case is the word *Esh* or "fire."

And the moral of all this?

When God, that is the hallowed and the ideal, is removed from the relationship of a man with a woman they are both transformed into consuming fires.

But when God is present between them their humanity is intact; man is man, woman woman, and both truly husband and wife to each other.


## 8. BETWEEN MAN AND HIS FELLOW

I owe myself respect for the divinity with which I am touched and for the singularity of my being.

But my neighbor is exactly in my case. He too is a child of God and equally unique.

Therefore, when I inquire as to my duties to my fellow I can accept only one answer: I may not withhold from him, or to permit others to withhold any of the reverence, solicitude, and freedom I claim for myself.

To this obligation there are no exceptions. Since all men

partake of God with me, I may exclude none from my deference, not by reason of race, creed, color, social position, economic class, or any other consideration.

To this obligation further there are no limits. I cannot respect my fellow excessively. On the contrary, since he contains something of God, his moral worth is infinite.

Translated into concrete terms, this means that I may not use him as a mere tool for my purposes but must always treat him as an end in himself. I may not injure him in any fashion, oppress, exploit, humiliate him, or deprive him of anything to which he is entitled. Nor may I deceive him or withhold the truth from him, since, as the rabbis pointed out long ago, oppression may be through words as well as deeds. Finally, I may not restrain or inhibit his self-fulfillment according to his talents, inclinations, and conscience.

In all this I have the right to expect him to behave toward me as I seek to behave toward him. No less a child of God than I, he is no more. "A man," say the rabbis, "is his own next of kin." If then I ought to stand in defense of his rights and dignities I should stand no less resolutely in defense of my own.

By Jewish lights, I am under no obligation to turn the other cheek, especially not if I have been unjustly slapped to begin with. The theory that evil should be endured rather than resisted has always been honored more in the breach than in practice, even by its official proponents. An unnatural principle, it is, in the Jewish view, also immoral in that it urges acquiescence in injustice. And injustice is never to be acquiesced in, no matter whom or where it strikes, not even if it strikes me.

In one situation only, according to the Tradition, ought I to submit to injury: when the sole alternative is my inflicting injury on an innocent third party. Accordingly, Jewish law ordains, a man shall prefer to die rather than to commit murder.

My ethical problem, however, is not normally a choice as bizarre as this. It is more likely to be the simpler business of making sure that I do right by others.

In this one word is the upshot of the Jewish teaching on what I owe my fellows: I owe them the *right*, the just, the equitable.

Even as it is written: "Righteousness, righteousness, shalt thou pursue."

But I am not yet done with my neighbor. Along with the fact that each of us is an isolated refraction of Deity, all of us are related manifestations of Him. Separated by our uniqueness, we are yet bound together by a high common descent. However deep our differences, the unity runs deeper; no matter how fierce our conflicts, our kinship is stronger still. For we are brothers in God.

Wherefore, over and beyond all else, I owe my neighbor the affections of brotherhood: sympathy in his distress, tolerance for his frailties, insight into his purposes, assistance in his aspirations, and, always, forbearance and peaceableness.

In sum, I owe him love, according to the precept: "Thou shalt love thy neighbor as thyself."

But is love properly a matter of obligations? Can it be enacted by statute, even by statute of Scripture? Is it not rather something spontaneous and uncalculated, a free-will offering quite detached from considerations of debt and duty?

So it is. But the *works* of love, as distinct from its mood, can be willed. Better of course the deed warmed by the spirit, but in any case, the deed.

As the Talmud points out time and again, many a good work undertaken out of dry-as-dust dutifulness has somehow ended up aglow with ardor. Indeed, one of the recurrent theses of Jewish moralistic literature is just this: that the best way to superinduce inner virtue is to behave virtuously.

To this purpose, the mystics of Safed in the sixteenth century banded together in ethical fellowships and adopted regimens of loving-kindness beyond the requirements of the Tradition, hoping that by additional labors of mercy and self-sacrifice the temper of compassion would be strengthened within them.

In this spirit an eighteenth century Jewish pietist, Joel son of Abraham Shemariah, counseled his children in his last testament:

> When in the course of worship you come to the "Sanctification" prayer . . . give especial thought to fulfilling the duty of loving your fellowman as yourself. For, in this "Sanctification" prayer we recite: "We will sanctify Thy name in the world, even as they [that is, the ministering angels] sanctify it in the heavens on high!" We undertake therefore to imitate the celestial beings and to comport ourselves in perfect love and harmony as they do.

> To this end, I have often made it my practice, when I found myself in an assemblage, to look over those present one by one, to ask myself whether in truth I loved everyone, whether indeed my acceptance of the command to love my fellow was genuine. With God's help I often found such to be the case. Whenever I noticed one who had done me some wrong I made it my rule to forgive him at that very instant, undertaking to love

him nevertheless. But if my heart refused to allow me to love him, then I would force myself to say great goodnesses concerning him until I had removed rancor from my heart.

And so, on any occasion when I met a man unto whom my heart did not incline, I would invoke blessings upon him to turn my heart to good concerning him and to the love of him.

In these lines saintliness speaks, with the simplicity and exaltation which normally attend it.

Now of saintliness and its devices only saints are capable. But in this counsel of Rabbi Joel, underneath its elevation there is a homely truth also, one attainable even by those who are less than saints: that while love comes at times uninvited and unplanned-for, it can often be induced by the simple expedient of doing its works.

## 9. MORALITY FOR SOCIETY

The Tradition holds that moral principles apply to societies as to men.

Like an individual, a community may be righteous or wicked, is liable to reward and punishment, may stand in need of expiation.

That is why long ago it was the wont of the High Priest on the Day of Atonement first to seek God's pardon for his own offenses and those of the priestly tribe, but then also on behalf of the whole House of Israel.

Hence, to the present time Jews pray on the same solemn occasion for remission of communal transgressions as well as those private.

To say that sin is communal means that the area of personal morality is much larger than is usually supposed. It signifies that every person, old enough to know what is going on in the world and strong enough to do something about it, is responsible more or less directly for every injustice committed by the state, economy, family, class, or institution in which he participates.

He may be guilty of acts of commission, of promoting and benefiting directly from the wrong. At the best he will be chargeable with the sin of nonfeasance described by the rabbis under the formula: "It was in their power to protest and they protested not."

The Tradition teaches further that the morality appropriate to the community is *mutatis mutandis* none other than that proper to the individual.

Society, equally with a human being, is under the following obligations:

—To take cognizance of the divinity resident in men by protecting them against oppression and according them the justice and freedom which are their due;

—To treasure their uniqueness by helping them to discover and realize their special gifts;

—To treat them as the equals they are before God.

—To translate into social actuality their oneness and brotherhood by fostering good will among them, by caring adequately for the weak and unfortunate, and by so ordering communal affairs as to foster peaceableness over violence and cooperation over competitiveness.

One other moral principle touches societies, not uniquely—since it pertains to individuals too—but in a special degree. That is an obligation as to the disposition of wealth.

According to the Tradition, the resources of nature and society constitute a gift bestowed by God on the whole human family for the purpose of enhancing the general welfare. This is not to deny an individual the right to own what he owns and to enjoy its fruits. Judaism approves of the institution of private property. But the right of possession is contingent on the faithful discharge of the terms of the trusteeship implicit in all ownership.

Let the state say what it will; as a matter of morality no one is entitled to withhold wealth from use, to destroy it by wastefulness or caprice, or to employ it against the collective interest. And it is society's duty, Judaism insists, to see to it that such abuses of possession are prevented, to guarantee that the world's goods are administered as God intended, for the good of mankind as a whole.

Judaism's doctrine of charity is in no slight measure a corollary to its attitude toward property.

Few social virtues are so highly lauded in traditional Jewish literature as philanthropy. Here furthermore the Jewish spirit has done some of its boldest and most creative pioneering. It thought out the ethic of charity, working out its practical applications so early and so well as to anticipate by centuries, even by millennia, many of the theories and techniques of modern social work.

This extraordinary preoccupation with charity represents in part the work of compassion, both the impulse common to all men and the conscious ideal inculcated and underscored by the Tradition.

But it is more than that. The poor man, religiously regarded, is, like any other man, the child of God. Yet through his poverty he has been disinherited from his patrimony in the world's goods. He is then no object of mere pity. He is a man denied his rights, among them that to an adequate livelihood.

Something must be amiss with society or such an inequity could not be. Charity, therefore is more than compassion; it is the rectification of communal failure.

Wherefore among the Hebrew words for charity the most common is *Zedakah,* which means not only assistance to the poor, but *righteousness.* For in aiding the distressed the community recaptures something of its lost integrity.

### 10. MAN THE CITIZEN

"Separate not thyself from the community," Hillel taught, giving classic expression to an important negation and an equally important affirmation, both deeply characteristic of the Tradition.

The negation is Judaism's opposition to any attempt on the part of men to isolate themselves from the generality of mankind.

The affirmation is its insistence on whole-hearted participation in the social enterprise as indispensable to the fulfillment of the human spirit.

To be sure, there have been periods in Jewish history when under stress of extraordinary circumstances Jews, either as individuals or in groups, renounced the world. One such juncture was the century or more immediately preceding the beginning of the Common Era. Then, in the Essenee sect of Palestine and the Egyptian-Jewish Therapeutae as described by Philo, Judaism developed a monasticism of its own, destined to serve subsequently as pattern and precedent for the early Christian anchorites and monachal orders. A similar tendency asserted itself, though less vigorously and effectively, in the mystical practices of the sixteenth century Kabbalists and in the phenomenon persisting almost to our day of the *Parush*, the "separated" one; that is, the man who though maintaining minimal family ties and social obligations still consecrates his life primarily to religious study, worship, and meditation.

Jews, in other words, have on occasion been attracted by the ideal of a secluded and cloistered existence; they have even, though not frequently, succumbed to its temptations. But Judaism in its main stream has not only never condoned hermitism, it has condemned it. The condemnation furthermore covers both types of withdrawal from the community: that whereby a person removes himself bodily from its midst, and that also in which he remains physically among his fellows but systematically blocks them and their concerns from his heart.

In the eyes of the Tradition, the recluse of either stripe is both immoral and unwise.

At the least he is an ingrate. Everything he is, needs, and uses—life, language, tools, ideals—has come to him from society. Having accepted these benefits at its hands, it is wrong for him to yield nothing in return.

He must, furthermore, despite his apparent idealism, be something of an egoist, one so concerned with saving his own spiritual neck that he feels no obligation to try to keep others from breaking theirs.

Again, it is when the world is most torn by conflict that the sheltered existence seems most appealing. But this is also the hour when humanity is most in need of intrepid hearts and skilled hands, of those who are capable of "turning back warfare from the very gates."

Nor is he distinguished for insight, since he overlooks the

so obvious truth that the individual and the community are inextricably bound together in a common fate.

To which point the rabbis spin one of their most incisive parables:

It happened once that men sat together in a boat at sea. Whereupon one of them drew forth an awl and began to bore into the boat's bottom.

"Stupid one," the others cried at him, "what are you doing?"

"And what concern is it of yours?" he answered. "Is it not under my own seat that I am making a hole?"

Finally, the tactic of escape is quite unlikely to attain that deliverance for which it is most often recommended, the fact being that if mankind be sick morally one may flee ever so far in the desert and still be overtaken by the plague. He who is solicitous over the health of his soul has no other course except to see to the health of his community.

Which is the moral read by the ancient rabbis into the wording of God's command to Moses as he stood in glory on Sinai while Israel in the valley below worshiped its golden calf: "Go, get *thee* down, for thy *people* . . . have become corrupt."

But all this is the dark side of the shield, a melancholy contention that we ought to identify ourselves with our communities *faute de mieux*, because there is no escaping them or because it is wrong or unwise to attempt to do so.

The social life, however, from the viewpoint of the Tradition, is no lesser of two evils. It is a good in itself, something inherently desirable and constructive.

There are joys which only companionship can yield, virtues that blossom only out of shared experience, and ideals that can be realized only in collectivity.

To do God's will, which requires of us justice, mercy, and humility, we must live with, among, and for other men.

If we are to show forth His glory and sanctify His name our fellows must be present with us; otherwise we shall have neither spectators nor audience.

Certainly the building of His Kingdom on earth pre-supposes our involvement in society, since the Kingdom, as we shall see later, is in the main our own society perfected and regenerated.

Here then is the heart of Judaism's insistence on full-blooded participation in group life. Without it man denies himself happiness, is hampered in his humanity, and debarred from the discharge of his human role. Or to put the matter in completely positive terms, he must bear himself warmly and well as a kinsman, congregant, citizen, and human being in order to find life worth while, to be true to his nature, and to advance God's design.

## II. THE SHADOW OF SIN

Highly as Judaism appraises man, it has no illusions concerning him. It knows full well that his character includes a great capacity for depravity; that his "wickedness is great in the earth, and that every imagination of the thoughts of his heart is only evil continually"; that his "heart is deceitful above all things and exceedingly weak." It is aware, in other words, of his moral infirmity, of the fact, to paraphrase God's word to Cain, that sin is ever at his door and unto him is its desire.

As to what it is in which sin consists the Tradition is altogether explicit.

The Jewish religion, as we have just finished observing, has very definite notions as to the nature of the good, both the general conception and its concrete applications.

Sin, in a word, is to be or do the opposite of the good. More specifically, it is any act or attitude whether of omission or commission which nullifies God's will, obscures His glory, profanes His name, opposes His Kingdom, or transgresses the *Mitzvoth* of the Torah. An even more detailed description of sin can readily be conjured up. The reader need only review the preceding chapters in this section on "The Good Life" and prefix a minus sign to every principle mentioned therein. When he is through he will have before him a fairly adequate catalogue of the deeds, moods, and thoughts which Judaism regards as sinful.

But why should sin be? Why should men be disposed, as they too often are, to spurn the good and prefer the evil?

To this difficult problem, the Tradition has and can have no single solution.

For sin is one specialized instance of evil, being evil as it resides in human nature and conduct. If then Judaism includes diverse explanations of evil in general it must embrace diverse theories of man's embodiment of it. The logical sequence is relentless: the Jewish religion propounds no single envisagement of God; it can therefore set forth no official justification of Him and His ways; it can therefore advance no exclusively acceptable doctrine as to sin. Indeed, as each theology projects a theodicy, so each theodicy implies its own account of sin and implies it so clearly that we need not tarry longer over the matter. If the reader will re-examine the many theodicies listed in the chapter entitled "The Great Shadow" he will have but slight difficulty in framing for himself the different Jewish interpretations of sin.

With sin as with evil the Tradition is far more concerned that men shall act rightly than that they shall speculate in some approved fashion.

Wherefore its first instruction concerning sin is that the impulse toward it and the habit of it can be resisted. Man is at core a free agent, the master in essentials of his own decisions. The very Scriptural verse which asserts that sin crouches ever at the door concludes with the assurance: "Yet mayest thou rule over it."

But since sin is resistable Judaism urges next: let a man resist it with all the vigor at his command. If temptation is hydra-headed, so also are the defenses against it. Among the time-tested strategies to this end especially recommended by the Tradition are reflection, prayer, the study of Torah and other religious and moralistic literatures, absorption in good works, the companionship especially of the wise and upright, and, first, last, and always, the exercise of will power.

Nor is sin, once committed, necessarily irremediable. Any injury it has inflicted on another may be reparable, or, failing that, subject to being compensated for. As for the harm it has done the sinner himself, this too may be made good at least in part through remorse and self-reform.

Past mistakes can often be retrieved. But never altogether —and sometimes not at all. When Cain murdered his brother, the Tradition points out, he slew not only Abel but Abel's unborn children. Not by any exertion on his part and not to the end of time could he right that wrong. There is a sense, let it be admitted, in which men abide forever under the shadow of their mistakes, paying for their errors every day of their lives and, through others, to all eternity.

And yet neither the world nor man is altogether the prisoner of the past. Reprieves can be won through the spiritual maneuver of repentance or atonement. Under either name this consists in two simultaneous endeavors: one external, the other internal.

The penitent must struggle first of all to mitigate the objective consequences of his error. Even when he can do next to nothing to that purpose, he must do the little he can.

At the same time, the penitent is required to work on his own soul in such a fashion as to superinduce two antithetical, almost paradoxical, effects.

He must seek to bring home to himself an open-eyed understanding of the causes, nature, and effects of his misdeeds, so that his remorse may be deep-seated and his will to betterment firm.

Having achieved this—in the very process of achieving it—he must take care that he shall not be crushed under his consciousness of wrongdoing but shall be able to go forward with good cheer and confidence.

The memory of old evils will and should remain with him; the sense of guilt will persist. But with time something else will emerge: a conviction of having won through to regeneration, to a recaptured oneness with moral values and the God behind them. This is the experience which the ancient rabbis knew and voiced when they portrayed God as saying to penitents: "Inasmuch as ye have come before Me in judgment and departed from before Me in peace, I do reckon it unto you as if ye had been created anew." This is the "returning" implied by *teshubah*, the classic Hebrew term for repentance.

To the rule that men are susceptible to sin the Tradition recognizes no exception.

Perfection is not a human trait.

To be totally free from error and evil is simply not possible to men. The good they seek is infinite and recedes infinitely from them; their vision is dim, their grasp feeble, their gait faltering. How can it be conceived of even the strongest and most ardent among them that he shall not fail in part?

Nor, according to the Tradition, has perfection ever been attained by anyone, not even by the saint or prophet. All transgressed and suffered moral defeat; the saint less, the sinner more, but all in some measure. And lest it be imagined that such a one as Moses, the servant of God so faithful in His house, may have escaped the universal fallibility of mankind, the Torah-Book says explicitly that he erred, in what he erred, and how he was punished.

What is more, Judaism does not expect perfection from man. There are religions which insist that he achieve it or be lost. Having set an unreachable standard, they foredoom him to damnation, from which only divine grace can deliver him. But since grace by definition is conferred, not won, God's intervention on his behalf comes out in the end unpredictable, even capricious. In this respect Judaism is mellower, more realistic. It thinks too well of God to portray Him as exacting impeccability from flesh and blood He has made frail. It is too sensible to ask that man walk but never slip. To the contrary it predicts that he will not only slip but fall also. Its guidance is directed to the end that he shall so walk as to fall as little as possible, and, having fallen, will pick himself up, brush off the dust and go on, wiser, surer of himself and of the good he seeks.

And may not this be the point of that cryptic tale in the

Book of Genesis, the story of how in the deep night Jacob
wrestled with an angel, prevailed against him, but was
wounded in the encounter; so that when the sun rose and he
went on his way he limped, and yet was crowned with a
new name and a fresh blessing in token of his victory?

Do we not also wrestle with life and sustain wounds because of which we limp painfully ever after, and yet, having
won out, bear with us names signifying increased honor and
benediction?

## 1. ISRAEL——TRADITIONALIST CONCEPTIONS

Judaism, the faith of Israel, includes also a faith *in* Israel, in the significance of the role of the Jewish people in history.

For the traditionalist that faith embraces four articles: the Election, the Covenant, the Mission, and the Vindication in time-to-come.

The Election is the doctrine that God chose Israel out of all the nations of the world to be the recipient of His revelation, the central figure in the drama of human salvation.

Why this people in particular?

In part because of the merits of the first fathers, whose righteousness was so great as to win this high calling for their descendants.

In part also because, according to one rabbinic theory, only this people was willing to accept the disciplines and hardships incidental to being elected. In this point, an ancient legend relates that God, when He was about to reveal the Torah, offered it in turn to every nation on earth, only to have it spurned because of its exacting moral demands. Israel alone received it and then, as the tale continues wryly in one version, less out of heroism than impetuosity.

The Covenant is the agreement between God and Israel.

As the word implies, the agreement is bilateral. If God selected Israel, Israel consented to be selected, and in that fact may be said not only to have been chosen by God, but to have chosen Him in turn.

Under the terms of their mutual understanding, Israel as one contracting party undertakes to do God's will without reckoning cost or consequence. God, for His part, makes Israel His particular treasure, a people near to Him.

No more exalted honor can be conceived than the Election. But it bestows no special privileges. Quite the reverse. It entails obligations and hardships.

More, not less, is expected of Israel by virtue of its unique station. Tribes ignorant of God and His will or uncommitted to them may be forgiven impieties and sins. Not so a kingdom of priests and a holy nation which has given its solemn, pledged word: "All that the Lord hath spoken will we do and obey." Wherefore the prophet warns the Jewish people in God's name:

> You only have I known of all the families of the earth;
> Therefore I will visit upon you all your iniquities.

What is more, peril, not security, attends the Election. The protagonist of justice and mercy must expect the assault of wicked men, the hostility of evil institutions. Against him the powers of darkness cannot but conspire to blot out his name, to silence his truth.

Such are the terms of the Covenant. They make a hard bargain, committing a people for all time to the role portrayed in the latter chapters of Isaiah, that of God's servant, willing to suffer if only he may serve.

But to what end the service?

Which query leads to the doctrine of the Mission.

Israel lives not merely to know God and do His will but, by preachment and example, to communicate His truth and way to the nations, so that blind eyes may be opened, the prisoners come forth from dungeons, and in the end all men be induced to form one band to do the right with a perfect heart.

The goal and final objective of the Mission are then none other than the deliverance of mankind. But in that happy event, when it has come to pass, what will be the servant's portion?

Israel will be present at the dénouement to experience his Vindication. His time of service ended, his commission discharged, he will partake, as he deserves, of the universal redemption he has labored so mightily to bring to pass.

His children, so long dispersed and persecuted, will be reassembled in their ancient land, there to enjoy peace and security proportionate to the bitterness and length of their exile.

The Jewish religion, so long mocked at and scoffed, will be universally recognized as the true faith.

The ruined Temple in Jerusalem will be rebuilt to stand as a house of prayer for all nations.

It is a glowing justification which the traditionalist foresees for Israel. But here too—and nothing could be more typical of the Jewish spirit—not the Jewish people alone comes into its own but all men with it; its deliverance being, when all is said and done, a part, essential but still a part, of the redemption of the whole human family.

## 2. ISRAEL——MODERNIST REINTERPRETATION

Modernists have done a quite thorough job of reworking the traditional conception of the Jewish people, rejecting some of it outright and accepting the rest only with radical alterations.

In their eyes, the doctrines of the Election, Covenant, Mission, and Vindication are all to be explained naturalistically as the projections of historical forces. To construe them so does not necessarily impugn their validity; it does, however, set them in a drastically different light.

All ancient peoples, modernists point out, assumed themselves to be chosen of their gods, such a belief on the part of Jews being, to begin with, only one instance of a universal notion. Yet the Jewish conception speedily became unique. No other nation of antiquity ever came to the point of regarding itself as chosen not for its own advantage but for service.

But why did the Jews alone reach this elevation? Because, modernists respond, of two factors: the first and more potent, the genius of the prophets; the second, the misfortunes that befell the Jewish community of Palestine. Zealous that all things should advance God's design, the prophets came inevitably to look on their own people as dedicated to that purpose. At the same time, the military defeats, poverty, and political precariousness of the Jewish state inclined Jews to seek their group *raison d'être* in directions other than conquest and prosperity.

When first conceived and for long afterward, the notion of Israel as a chosen people had substantial warrant in facts. In all the ancient world only the Jews possessed a tenable

God-faith, a humane morality, and a hope for the human future.

The rise of Christianity and Mohammedanism gave further corroboration to the Jewish claim to Election, for both these religions viewed Israel as the original chosen people which had, however, subsequently forfeited its distinction. The Jew naturally accepted from the Gentiles the testimony favorable to himself and disregarded the rest.

Then, in the Middle Ages, the doctrine of the Election took on heightened importance for Jews, supplying them with self-respect, purposefulness, and confidence at a time when the whole world conspired to dispirit them and break their strength.

This is the outline story of the evolution of the Election, Covenant, Mission, and Vindication as modernists reconstruct it.

But what of the present validity of these doctrines?

Here modernists disagree among themselves.

Some hold that, while such ideas may once have had a reason for being and may even have been true in a fashion, they ought no longer to be retained: first, because they draw invidious contrasts between Israel and the nations; and second, because these contrasts are no longer factually defensible, the Jews these days being no more conspicuous for dedication to God's purposes than some other groups.

The typical modernist is less radical on the issue. He denies outright any interest in drawing contrasts, an occupation he finds distasteful. But he is not so ready to forget the history of the idea of the Election or so indifferent to its potential future uses.

He points out that in literal fact the Jews were the first to choose God in the sense of consecrating themselves to

Him. They constitute therefore the original chosen people. Then, too, they have consistently made the doing of His will their collective purpose. Wherefore they may be said to have been a chosen people continuously. And as for the present, they may, if they so will it, go on with their historic role. They need only dedicate themselves, as did their fathers, to God's law and design. Let them choose Him once more, and they are again chosen. The Election lives, the Covenant is in force, the Mission goes forward, and the Vindication waits the predestined moment. Israel is as always the servant of God.

So holds the right-wing modernist.

But, one asks, what of the other peoples of the world?

Let them, too, choose God, he answers, and they also are chosen.

### 3. LAND AND LANGUAGE

Judaism looks upon Palestine and the Hebrew tongue as sacred.

They are sacred, both of them, for their associations. It was in the Holy Land and in Hebrew that revelation came to the prophets and was imparted by them to Israel and mankind. Palestine was the site of many of the supremely memorable incidents in Jewish history, and Hebrew was the medium for most of the precious utterances of the Jewish soul. One cannot revere the Tradition without coming by transference to revere the idiom in which it spoke and the earth from which it sprang.

Both are sacred for the uses to which they are put. It is in Hebrew that a Jew prays, worships, and conducts his spiritual exercises, entirely if he be a strict traditionalist, in part large or small if a modernist. In either case at every high moment in his spiritual career some Hebrew phrase is likely to be sounded.

Similarly the consciousness of Palestine pervades every phase of his religious life. The Scripture he reads, the prayers he recites, the rabbinic literature he studies are full of allusions to it. And as for Jewish rites and observances, having been fashioned in the Holy Land, they reflect their native scene. Like other faiths Judaism takes cognizance of the cycle of the seasons. But the calendar it follows is Palestinian in form and inspiration. Passover marks the ripening of the first grain, Pentecost the garnering of the first fruits, Tabernacles the final ingathering—all as they occur in the Holy Land. Always Palestine sets the pitch of Judaism's awareness of the agricultural and pastoral.

Land and language are sacred, last of all, for their place in the vision of the future.

Except for extreme modernists, all religious Jews regard Palestine and the Hebrew tongue as involved in some fashion in the destiny of Israel and mankind.

Many a traditionalist believes that the reconstitution of Israel on its ancestral soil is a precondition to the Messianic era. When the dispersed Jews of the world have been brought home by the Messiah, Torah will go forth from Zion, the word of the Lord from Jerusalem, swords will be beaten to plowshares and spears to pruning hooks.

Less rigid traditionalists and the bulk of modernists see the future in a less mystical light. To them Palestine and the Hebrew language contribute in natural course to the triumphant outcome of the human adventure.

For long centuries the growth of Judaism has been hampered by dispersion and persecution. But when a Jewish Commonwealth has come into being, when outcast Jews have found peace, when the Hebrew language and literature have taken root in their native soil, the Tradition will have a fresh chance at free, spontaneous unfolding. Its circumstances will be favorable as they have not been in two millennia. And not in Palestine only, but throughout the world. For Palestine then will be an unfettered heart pumping the blood of health and vigor to all the Jewries of the dispersion.

Who knows what revelations the people of revelations shall have to speak at that time? This much is certain: the Jewish people everywhere will be the stronger for the Homeland and its revived Hebrew culture, and therefore the better able to labor for the advent of that ideal society which it was the first to project and after which it has striven so long and mightily.

### 4. NON-JEWS

According to the Tradition, all men, regardless of race, religion, or nationality are equally God's children, equally precious in His sight, equally entitled to justice and mercy at the hands of their fellows. Except by virtue of character and conduct, no man is better than any other.

Wherefore, Judaism claims no superiorities whatsoever for Jews, at least none that are inherent to them. It does assert that they enjoy certain advantages, the nature of their religious heritage, for example, or what the ancient rabbis used to call "the merits of the fathers"; that is to say, the group patrimony of faith and goodness accumulated through the ages and available to each new generation. But these are social, cultural advantages which have to be accepted and exploited by the individual, or they are of no account. Neither in them nor anywhere else in the Jewish religion is there the least suggestion of sanction for theories of racial superiorities and inferiorities.

Judaism indeed is totally unaware of race. Though the Tradition loves to trace the House of Israel to the Patriarchs, blood descent is no factor in its calculations. Anyone accepting the Jewish faith becomes "a child of Abraham our father" and a "son of Israel" of equal worth with all others. Nor is anyone debarred from conversion because of national or ethnic origins. Judaism has high standards for the admission of proselytes, but they are entirely theological, ethical, ritualistic, and educational.

Anyone may become a Jew; but no one has to do so in order to be saved, whether in this world or the next.

The Tradition rules explicitly: "The righteous of all peoples have their share in the world to come."

On which very consequential point Judaism stands in sharp contrast to historic Christianity.

The universalism of the Christian religion has been frequently commented on, the fact that in its eyes and according to the teaching of Paul: "There is neither Jew nor Greek, there is neither bond nor free, there is neither male nor female: for ye are all one in Christ Jesus. And if ye be Christ's, then are ye Abraham's seed, and heirs according to the promise."

But what is often overlooked in Paul's preachments is the explicit condition he imposes, namely, "*If ye be Christ's.*" Paul's universalism applies to professing Christians only, and of them only to those who profess correctly, that is, in harmony with Paul's ideas. All other men, no matter how truth-loving, devout, and good are irretrievably damned. Or to put the thesis in Paul's own unmistakable words: "He that disbelieveth shall be condemned."

Nor is it only Paul who limits salvation to Christians who subscribe to some special set of articles of faith.

Such is exactly the position of Roman Catholicism: *extra ecclesiam nulla salus*, "outside the church there is no salvation."

Except for its radical sects, the case with Protestantism is quite similar.

Rejecting such exclusiveness, Judaism holds that any righteous person may expect whatever rewards accrue to righteousness in this world or the next.

Indeed, from the strictly traditionalist viewpoint, there is a sense in which Gentiles come by salvation more easily than Jews (though not so certainly). For of a non-Jew it is required only that he conform to the "seven commandments ordained upon the sons of Noah" which are the principles of piety and morality conceived by the ancient rabbis as binding on all mankind: to refrain from (1) idolatry; (2) incest and adultery, (3) bloodshed; (4) the profanation of God's name; (5) injustice and lawlessness; (6) robbery; and (7) inhumane conduct, such as cutting a limb from a living animal. What is more, Talmudic literature is studded with incidents concerning heathens who are said "to have acquired the world to come" by single acts of extraordinary kindness and integrity. Against that, it is expected of Jews for their salvation that they shall undertake to discharge as many of the six hundred and thirteen commandments of the Torah as apply to them.

Judaism's readiness to recognize that others aside from Jews possess spiritual merit sufficient for salvation constitutes an instance of liberalism almost unique in western theology.

It helps also to account for the position taken by the Jewish religion on converts, the fact that it will accept but not seek them, that indeed rabbis are instructed to dissuade would-be proselytes, receiving them only if they persist in their intention.

This unusual, almost paradoxical, attitude is in some measure the product of history. Once, in the days of the Roman Empire, the Jews engaged in missionary activity energetically and on a wide scale; some of them even dreamed of converting the whole heathen world. But many of the hard-won pagans hankered after the ways they had ostensibly abandoned and were forever trying to insinuate them into Judaism. Many proved to be fair-weather believers, deserting their new faith as soon as it became an object of persecution. Many went over to other, ritually less exacting religions, notably Mithraism and Christianity. Once burned, twice careful. The present-day Jewish rule as to converts was designed to make sure of their earnestness and constancy.

Even more, it implements the conviction that any good person, Jew or non-Jew, is acceptable before the Lord. Judaism lacks the postulate which serves as mainspring to the proselytizing zeal of other communions. It does not assume that it alone can save from eternal damnation.

The breadth of the Jewish outlook appears the more remarkable when one reflects on the frequent and savage persecutions to which Jews were subjected all through the Middle Ages. It would have been understandable, in view of their experiences, had they entertained the ambition ascribed to them by Shakespeare of executing the villainy they had been taught and bettering the instruction, or had they denied all possibility of salvation to any member of the church that tormented them. That they continued to believe that any good man merits eternal bliss speaks volumes for Judaism and the idealism of medieval Jews.

### 5. OTHER RELIGIONS

To the Jewish traditionalist Judaism is religion *par excellence, the* true faith.

Other religions however are not necessarily or totally false. On the contrary they may be true in part, according to the degree in which they approximate Judaism.

By this criterion, non-Jewish communions run a gamut from the altogether benighted to the almost completely enlightened. Idolatry and polytheism are outright superstition and error. In trinitarian Christianity valid and invalid elements commingle. And a fellowship of ethical monotheism such as Unitarianism is unexceptionable as far as it goes, except that it does not go far enough.

A clear statement of the traditionalist outlook on this point is contained in the Eighth Canto of the eleventh century poem, *The Royal Crown* by Solomon ibn Gabirol.

Thou art God, and all things formed are Thy servants and worshipers.
Yet is not Thy glory diminished by reason of those that worship aught beside Thee,
For the yearning of them all is to draw nigh Thee.
But they are like the blind,
Setting their faces forward on the King's highway,
Yet still wandering from the path.
One sinketh into the well of a pit
And another falleth into a snare,
But all imagine they have reached their desire,
Albeit they have suffered in vain.
But Thy servants are as those walking clear-eyed in the straight path,

Turning neither to the right nor the left
Till they come to the court of the King's palace.

In the foregoing quotation the reader should observe, first, the clear ascription to *all* men of a genuine desire for God; second, the Pilgrim's Progress, as it were, of the various religions wherein some travel the King's highway further than others; and finally the confidence that only Judaism reaches to the palace. Here, in a parable, is the traditionalist doctrine.

Modernists refuse to look on the diverse communions as though they were so many systems of propositions of which only one can be true while all others must be false. They conceive of them rather as one thinks of different individuals or cultures, each possessed of verities and virtues peculiar to itself.

In this light, it is good, not regrettable, that religions are plural, just as it is advantageous to the world that there are many persons and civilizations.

Life is the richer in color and variety.

Each faith is stimulated by the others and is spurred constantly by their criticism to self-purification.

The different churches supplement one another, each contributing some insight or value peculiar to itself, or else putting a distinctive interpretation and hue onto propositions and ideals common to all. Thus the total life of the human spirit is more rounded than could be achieved from one source alone.

Individual doctrines are of course either true or false—an issue of burning moment. But no communion is of error all compact. In any case, religion is not an arithmetical process to be exploded by the discovery of a mistake. Nor ought the adherents of any faith to claim on its behalf all of truth and goodness. Rather is it their duty to make the most of its virtues, correct its fallacies, and make good its deficiencies.

For the Jewish modernist Judaism is wonderfully dowered with merits of the highest order: lucidity and reasonableness in doctrine, exaltation yet practicality in ethic, a passion for social justice, balance between body and soul, a wealth of poetic rituals, dedication to freedom of conscience, reverence for the life of reason, and others in addition.

But any religion may share in some of these qualities, or display still others which Judaism lacks.

Brahmanism has gone much further in exploring the mystic way and in evolving techniques of discipline.

Quakerism has worked out in greater detail the ethics of peaceableness.

Roman Catholicism is more elaborate and dramatic ritually.

The end of the matter is this: the Jewish modernist prefers not to put religions in contrast with one another. He is content that each has its share of verity and worth, that all have the right to be, that out of their diversity, God, man and the truth are better served in the long run.

As for himself, he is at peace in Judaism.

It is his own; he is bound to it as to his parents and native land.

It is the faith of the people of which he is a member.

It has an inexhaustible fund of special excellences.

It is unique and therefore irreplaceable. The world would be impoverished were it lost.

Wherefore he is satisfied to live in it, and, when his time comes, to die in it. It is enough for him, and more.

## 6. JUDAISM ON JESUS

The Jewish judgment of Christianity at any moment is the resultant of two factors, one a variable, the other a constant.

The variable is Christian conduct as it touches all men and things, Jews and Judaism not least among them. It is all very well to say that a cause must never be held chargeable for the deportment of its advocates. And no doubt some persons are strong minded enough to abide by this rule. Most people, being made of less heroic stuff, appraise theory, at least to some extent, by practice.

When the Christian conforms to the virtues he preaches, Jews in turn cannot but be favorably impressed with the faith that molds him. But when, as is unfortunately too often the case, he not only condones the persecution of Jews but takes a hand in it, when indeed clergymen and churches prove to be fierce instigators of anti-Semitism, then inevitably the respect of Jews for Christianity is adversely affected.

The constant in Judaism's appraisal of Christianity is the nature of Christianity itself, which for our purposes embraces two elements: the personality of Jesus, and the religion built on and about him.

What do Jews think of Jesus?

The very posing of this question raises flocks of problems logically anterior to it.

Whose Jesus are we talking about? Is it the supernatural Christ of the Byzantine and Roman churches who is so much God as to be man scarcely at all; or is it the flesh and blood Nazarene of Hicksite Quakerism or Unitarianism who is so very human as to be God little more than any other mortal?

The query is unanswerable for the reason that there is no one Jesus but many, according to the number of churches in Christendom. But let us circumvent the impasse by recasting our question. Let us ask: "What do Jews think of the Jesus of the Gospels?"

Even this inquiry is less simple than appears. The four Evangels are by no means at one in their portraitures of the Nazarene. Even when their discrepancies are overlooked, and they are sometimes grave, other difficulties remain. Are the miracles reported of Jesus in the New Testament irrelevant or integral to his message: that he raised the dead, walked on the water, exorcised demons who entered a herd of swine which then straightway rushed over a precipice into the sea, that he was born of a virgin, that having been dead three days he came to life again and mounted up to heaven? What is one to make of the conclusion of higher criticism that the Gospel books are to a considerable degree propaganda pieces, each of which shows traces of seeking to establish a thesis? But if some of the New Testament is suspect as to credibility and another part for tendentiousness what portion of it shall be accepted as factual?

Let us however suppress all such misgivings. Let us take the Gospel story as it stands, strain out of it the episodes that relate of wonderworking, and then ask what Judaism has to say of the Jesus who emerges, who is incidently the Jesus of many liberal Christians.

To Jews, that Jesus appears as an extraordinarily beautiful and noble spirit, aglow with love and pity for men, especially for the unfortunate and lost, deep in piety, of keen insight into human nature, endowed with a brilliant gift of parable and epigram, an ardent Jew moreover, a firm believer in the faith of his people; all in all, a dedicated teacher of the principles, religious and ethical, of Judaism.

But is he not something more than a teacher? Should he not be taken for a moral prophet also, one who promulgated new, higher, hitherto unknown principles of conduct?

Not if the record is examined objectively. The signal fact about Jesus is that except for some relatively unimportant details which we shall specify in a moment, he propounded no ethical doctrine in which the Jewish Tradition had not anticipated him. Indeed what he taught was the Jewish Tradition as he had received it from Scripture and the sages. For every principle he preached, for very many of the epigrams and parables he struck off, Biblical or rabbinic precedent exists. The very phrases of the Sermon on the Mount can be paralleled one by one from the Jewish devotional literature of his time.

Nor is it at all true that Jesus introduced the concepts of love and compassion into a Judaism that knew stern justice only. No one who considers the Old Testament can fail to perceive that ages before the Nazarene was born, mercy and love had been conceived in Israel and accepted as authentic and supreme virtues. Anyone who studies rabbinic literature will discover that the ideal of humaneness preached by Jesus, far from being peculiar to him, was the common aspiration of all good souls in his people and time.

This is not to deny Jesus' originality. His was an unexcelled gift for allegory, a genius for incisive utterance, a skill for bringing into sharp focus that which is perceived, but as through a glass, darkly. He had great talents as a synthesizer, a collector into organic unity of the disjointed members of a truth. And always there is his own personality, a superb achievement in its own right. All this is originality, but, except for the man himself, on a secondary or derivative plane. It consists not in *creatio ex nihilo* but in rearranging and furbishing that which is already acknowledged. The moral prophet, however, is an innovator, proclaiming a hitherto unsuspected verity. By this definition, Jesus, whatever else he may have been, was no prophet.

As was admitted, indeed, by Julius Wellhausen when he said: "Jesus was not a Christian; he was a Jew. He did not preach a new faith."

In only a few respects did Jesus deviate from the Tradition and in all of them, Jews believe, he blundered.

He would seem to have claimed to be the Messiah foretold by the prophets as the inaugurator of God's Kingdom on earth. The condition of the world since his advent has never impressed Jews as justifying such an appraisal of him.

Again, Judaism is jarred by the world-weariness he displayed, his indifference to social affairs and day-by-day living, his absorption in life after death and in the Messianic Era. This temper in him is easy to account for. Together with many Jews of his time, he seems to have been convinced that the end of the old order of nature and society was at hand, that a new and ideal age was soon to be inaugurated. What is more he expected this cosmic revolution in the lifetime of his followers. "This generation," he said, "shall not pass away till all be fulfilled." "There are some standing here that shall not taste of death till they see the Kingdom of God coming with power."

Given this conviction, given his otherworldliness, and many of his perplexing utterances become intelligible.

Of course he was unperturbed by the tyranny of the Roman Empire, and ready to "render unto Caesar the things that are Caesar's." (Substitute "Mussolini" for "Caesar" for the full impact of the saying.) First of all, his kingdom was not of this world. Let Roman conquerors then do with the earth as they chose. Besides, what was the sense in resisting Rome when, in a few short years, the old dispensation, the Empire included, would be wiped away by the all-powerful hand of God? Required of men then was not the courage to defy an evil order, but the patience to abide it until it disappeared.

In this light, one sees the logic behind his estimate of marriage when he lauds those "which make themselves eunuchs for the kingdom of heaven's sake"; his judgment on family life when he says, "There is no man that hath left house, or parents, or brethren, or wife, or children, for the kingdom of God's sake, who shall not receive manifold more in this present time, and in the world to come life everlasting"; his advice to his followers to "take no thought for your life, what ye shall eat or what ye shall drink." All these are counsels natural to one who has turned his back on the world to begin with and in addition believes the end of days to be at hand. But they are scarcely a livable instruction either for those who do not spurn life on earth or who expect society to endure longer than another generation.

But will not Jews accept him, if not as a prophet, then at the least as a perfect man, an ideal for all to imitate?

That too is not tenable. The sober truth is that Jesus, spiritual hero that he is, is not perfect. The ideal Jesus of the Christian imagination is actually an idealization, achieved by an unconscious but judicious selection from New Testament incidents.

Thus, Jesus shows no interest in the life of reason and beauty, more specifically in the philosophy, science, and

art of the Greco-Roman world of his time. If his outlook
is lofty, it is narrow.

Then, too, he is so preoccupied with the individual and
his salvation that he has little to say about society. Few of
the communal conflicts of his time touch him. He makes
no proposals about measures to abolish slavery, about the
rights of the free laborer and how they may be assured,
about the all-devouring statism of the Roman Empire and
how it is to be opposed. His *social* gospel is very slight, so
slight that Christendom has had to reach back of him to
the prophets of the Old Testament for its political and
economic ideals.

Nor was his character altogether unexceptionable.

He was capable of bursts of ill-temper, as when he cursed
the towns of Capernaum, Chorazin, and Beth Saida, or when
he denounced a fig tree for not yielding fruit to appease his
hunger, though it was not the fruit-bearing season. And he
was intemperate in his condemnation of the scribes and
Pharisees, most of whom were thoroughly honest and dedicated men.

Finally, there are at least traces of chauvinism in him.
When a Canaanite woman pleads with him to heal her daughter, he responds: "It is wrong to take the children's bread,
and throw it to the little dogs." He declares explicitly: "I
am not sent except to the lost sheep of the House of Israel."
To him "Gentile" and "publican" are equally terms of op-
probrium. And he plainly instructs the Apostles not to bear
his message to non-Jews.

These failings are understandable and pardonable as human
frailties. Certainly they are more than offset by virtues.
The point is, however, that they are inconsistent with any
claim to perfection on Jesus' behalf, with any suggestion

that he constitutes a paragon to be uncritically revered and emulated without reservation.

Very well then, says the Christian, let it be conceded that Jesus is neither God, nor uniquely His son, nor the Messiah, nor a moral prophet, nor even an impeccable human being.

Certainly he was, despite his defects, a great man, a gifted and exalted teacher. Will not the Jews accept him as such?

To which the answer of Jews runs: "Have Jews, except under the extremest provocation, ever quarreled with such a presentation of him?"

### 7. JUDAISM ON CHRISTIANITY

It was Paul who was mainly responsible for the emergence of Christianity as a new, distinct religion.

With the bulk of the ideas and ideals of Jesus Judaism, as we have seen, is in deep accord. How could it be otherwise when these ideas and ideals are its own? The disagreements are over a specific claim as to the Messiahship, over differences of moral emphasis and direction, over items which large as they loom are quite dwarfed when set against those shared. And except when Jews were embittered by savageries and indignities wrought upon them in Jesus' name, they were quite aware of the large community of tenet and purpose between him and themselves. In this spirit and with an objectivity to which the Christian world of his time showed no reciprocity Moses Maimonides paid tribute to Jesus as "one who prepared the way for the Messianic King."

With Paul, however, it was another story. Though he was "in the flesh," as he himself attests, "of the stock of Israel, of the tribe of Benjamin, a Hebrew of the Hebrews," he was very much a product of the Greco-Roman world. The Hellenist spirit ran strong in him, leading him eventually to an outlook and set of values radically incompatible with Judaism. Indeed, as the Book of Acts makes clear, his innovations were strongly resisted by the very Apostles who knew Jesus most intimately, especially by Peter and James, "brother of the Lord." Nevertheless, he succeeded in winning the Christian fellowship to his ideas. It is these Pauline elements in Christianity to which Judaism has objected ever since:

—The insistence that the flesh is evil and to be suppressed;

—The notion of original sin and damnation from before birth of all human beings;

—The conception of Jesus not as a man but as God made flesh;

—The conviction that men can be saved vicariously, that indeed this is the only fashion in which they can be saved, and that Jesus is God's sacrifice of his only begotten son so that by believing on him they may be saved;

—The abrogation of the authority of Scripture and the Tradition, and the nullification of the commandments of the Torah;

—The faith that Jesus, having been resurrected from the dead, bides his time in Heaven until the hour is come for him to return to earth to judge mankind and establish God's Kingdom;

—The final and climactic doctrine that he who earnestly believes these things is automatically saved, but that he who denies them, no matter how virtuous otherwise, is lost to eternal perdition.

These propositions and their corollaries Judaism repudiates. But since they are the warp and woof of historic Christianity, the rejection of them carries in its train the rejection of the Christian fabric as a whole.

The split between Christianity and Judaism was irreparable in the time of Paul and largely because of him. Once the two faiths broke away from each other they continued to diverge ever afterward, moving farther apart as Christian theology grew more and more elaborate, as it asserted the Trinity, the miracle of the mass, the cult of saints, the intercessive power of Mary, and the doctrinal infallibility of the Popes.

Now, Christianity is, of course, infinitely more than those of its tenets and traits to which Judaism objects. Furthermore, it is entitled to be judged in terms of its strengths rather than weaknesses. If we seem now to be concentrating on the latter, it is not out of blindness to the former. No thoughtful Jew can be other than admiring of the depth and brilliance of the great metaphysicians of Christendom, the sublimity of its moralists and saints, the genius of its liturgists, architects, artists, poets, and musicians, the heroism of its social reformers, and the simple goodness of multitudes of its faithful. At this moment, however, we are explaining Judaism's dissociation from Christianity. That was the result not of the virtues of the Christian heritage but of those elements in it of which the Jewish Tradition could not approve.

Will the gap be filled? Will the two religions, mother and daughter, ever be reconciled?

Of course, says the traditionalist Jew; when Christians put aside the amendments and additions to Judaism made by the church.

Yes, says the fundamentalist Christian, when Jews accept the Christ as their savior.

Many modernists in both camps see no reason why the two

faiths need coalesce. Let each be as pure and strong in its own character as it can. For the rest, there is need not for filling in gaps but for bridging them with mutual candor and understanding.

## 8. THE PARTICULAR AND THE UNIVERSAL

Judaism denies that there need be strain between the particular and the universal, the self and the community, a specific religion and spirituality, loyalty to Israel and allegiance to mankind.

It never asks whether man ought to exist for himself or for his fellows. It assumes that he will live for both, that he can best minister to other men by first realizing his own potentialities. Only—and this is the decisive proviso—the larger end must never be swallowed up in the smaller. Always the cultivation of self must be pointed, consciously and deliberately, to the overarching service of society and beyond that to God. So the excesses of individualism are obviated, not by denying individuality—an inane or destructive course—but by causing it to minister to broader interests.

By the same token, there is no antinomy between attachment to kin, people, nation, or faith and devotion to humanity as a whole. Judaism takes it for granted that a man will love his own passionately, yet it expects him to avoid the pitfalls of exclusiveness and intolerance. All by the simple device of subordinating the narrower to the wider devotions, until all minister to the widest, the world community and God's will.

Is Judaism itself to be taken for a universal religion or a particularistic, for something as broad as mankind or concentrated on a special group? The answer quite obviously is, both. Judaism is the particular faith of a particular people, but the people and faith alike are consecrated to the most comprehensive of ideals.

In which respect Judaism maintains a rare, perhaps unique, position. Men and communions are likely to slip into the blunder of setting loyalties apart from one another, of pitting the individual against the group, the nation or people against mankind, the church against the spirit. Having established a false antithesis, they then proceed to demand of men either that they forswear their natural attachments or, alternatively and even worse, that they betray the whole for the sake of the part.

Judaism wisely and realistically accommodates itself to the fact that men have many affiliations. It does not ask that they quit being unique persons, or members of groups, all for some hypothetical and utopian generalization. It insists rather that they shall be the best they can of their kind, as men, citizens, and communicants, making sure to consecrate that best to God and the world.

The particular and the universal are rivals no more. The former rather gives weight, concreteness, and momentum to the latter; the latter elevates the former and redeems it from parochialism.

# VII

## 1. THE BRIDGE OF PRAYER

Prayer is the bridge between man and God.

With the intellect one figures out that God *is* and also something of what He must be.

In intuition one experiences Him.

In revelation one receives testimony concerning Him, more or less definitive according to the credence given it.

In the good life one charts a course by His light.

In ritual one celebrates Him.

But only in prayer does one establish a soul to soul interchange with Him.

Prayer then consists in two elements: that a soul shall be oriented toward God; and that, whether with words or not, it shall address Him.

Since man turns to God in many moods and designs, prayers are equally numerous and diverse as to temper and purpose. Certain types, however, recur with high frequency, no doubt because they articulate common and elemental emotions.

Of these the most notable are:

—The prayer of *contemplation*, in which man meditates on God and His will;

—The prayer of *adoration*, in which the greatness and mystery of God are considered;

116

—The prayer of *thanksgiving*, in which, having experienced God's goodness, man puts into words his gratitude and indebtedness;

—The prayer of *affirmation*, which crystallizes the faith of the believer and his aspirations;

—The prayer of *resignation*, in which, his own devices and strength exhausted, man casts his burdens on the Lord;

—The prayer of *penitence*, wherein the guilty conscience confesses its guilt and appeals for purification from it;

—The prayer of *protest*, the pouring forth of human indignation against the injustices of the world and the voiced demand that they be set right;

—The prayer of *quest*, in which, lost and confused, man gropes for light and direction, sometimes for the very God to whom he addresses his supplications;

—The prayer of *petition*, in which the heart's desires are asked for, whether they be things physical or spiritual, whether for self or for others.

Of these major categories of prayer, examples can be found almost anywhere in life and letters but with extraordinary wealth and profusion in Scripture—the Book of Psalms in particular—in rabbinic literature, and especially in the established Jewish prayer books. If the reader, on completing this primer, will turn to these source texts, he will find in them fascinating instances of the shapes and powers of this tool of the spirit.

## 2. WORSHIP

Man is not himself only, he is a participant in his community. Hence it is not enough that he shall address God in his solitariness; he must turn to Him in his other aspect as well.

Man's prayer as a social being is worship.

Worship does not have to be public, though that is its most usual circumstance; nor need it follow a pre-established program as to text and rite, though it almost always does. Any prayer or ceremonial is worship if it voices either the community or a single person speaking as a member of the group.

The Tradition expects the Jew to set up his private relationship with God, to confront Him when and as the spirit moves him.

"Would that a man might pray the livelong day," was the hope of an ancient rabbi.

But a Jew is also an Israelite, a fellow in the Jewish people. Wherefore Judaism has established a schedule of times and seasons at which he shall come to God in this capacity. It has laid down the principles he shall affirm on such occasions, the ideals he shall assert, even the *personal* expectations which, being a Jew, he ought to entertain. It has gone so far as to work out the very words and ritual gestures in which all these are to be expressed. For this is the nature of the accepted Jewish prayerbooks for weekdays, Sabbaths, festivals, and holy days: they state the fundamental minimal aspirations required of a traditional Jew on his own behalf and cherished by Jewry as a collectivity.

### 3. PRECONDITIONS FOR PRAYER

Highly as the Tradition esteems prayer—indeed, *because* it values it so highly—it insists that it be discreetly used.

Prayer to be efficacious must be sincere. It must bespeak genuine, not pretended aspirations.

Prayer to be efficacious must be alive. The dead, mechanical mumbling of words is not prayer but a travesty.

Prayer to be efficacious must be predicated on true conceptions of God and reality. Not that only metaphysicians and theologians may pray. The simplest person possessed of the most naive notions has equal rights and privileges with anyone else—often, in his spiritual ingenuousness, greater. But there must be behind all errors and misconceptions some bit of valid insight, religious or moral.

Prayer to be efficacious must place God's will higher than man's and, when the two conflict, must subordinate the latter to the former. Always it must begin with the postulate, implied or expressed, "May it be Thy will." Always it must close with the thought, verbalized or silent, "Thy will be done."

Prayer to be efficacious must be ethical; not seeking what is contrary to moral principle; not setting the aspirations of any man above the equally legitimate aspirations of his fellow, or above the hopes of men in the mass.

It must come from one possessed of clean hands or from one earnestly desirous of becoming clean. A man shall not approach God while the spoil of the poor is hidden in his household or seek forgiveness for transgressions with the design of sinning again so soon as his prayers are done.

It must reach out for the highest and noblest, not the second-best, of which a man is capable.

Last of all, prayer to be efficacious must not seek the impossible. Of which abuse of prayer the Talmud quotes two telling examples:

A man whose wife is about to bear a baby shall not pray: "May it be Thy will that the child carried by my wife prove to be a boy [or a girl]." Such a prayer, say the rabbis, is nonsensical. For the unborn babe in actuality is already either a boy or a girl.

Again, the rabbis insist, a man who hears a fire alarm sounding in his city shall not pray: "May it be Thy will that the conflagration be not in my home." And that for two reasons: first, such a prayer asks in effect that the misfortune befall another, which is immoral; and second, the fire is already where it is.

In sum, a man shall not pray that facts be not facts.


### 4. THE EFFICACY OF PRAYER

Prayer to be efficacious . . .

But what according to the Tradition is the efficacy of prayer? Does it avail?

That God responds to prayer is a basic belief of Judaism.

On the extent of the response the Jewish faithful disagree, some being optimists or maximalists on the issue; others, if not pessimists, are at least circumspect or minimalist.

All Jews acknowledge the conditions and limits of prayer we have listed. Even the most sanguine concede further that it does not replace human effort. One should not address God, fold his hands, and wait for his wish to come true—at least not if one is true to Judaism. One prays but works, too. A sick man calls on God but on his physician also. Otherwise, the Tradition holds, he is a sinner against his own soul and against God who endowed the surgeon with his skill and the drugs with their properties.

Given the right use, prayer may, in the Jewish view, achieve the following:

It can first of all—and on this all religious Jews are agreed —release pent-up feelings, crystallize inarticulate thoughts, muster the will, and all in all prove of great psychological worth.

It can further—and on this too there is general assent—tap levels of personality otherwise not to be reached, setting free the full resources of the spirit.

On why prayer possesses this peculiar potency the circumspect and the optimists differ. The former contend that the process is purely naturalistic, being the very normal response of man's psyche to an idea as compelling as that of God. The latter are far bolder, holding that in prayer man is inundated by the divine; an experience quite beyond natural law and not to be accounted for by it.

All religious Jews agree next that prayer exerts an influence on things outside man. But once again there is disagreement on the *how*. The minimalists maintain that prayer sways the physical world only through human agencies. The maximalists insist that quite apart from man it impinges directly on reality.

Then, is the maximalist position that the sky, as it were, is the limit, that prayer can accomplish any result whatsoever?

On this point the maximalists themselves divide. Some argue that prayer must function within natural law as science describes it and that no accomplishment is to be awaited beyond its confines.

Others, super-maximalists as they may be called, contend that nature is but a tool in God's hand. Nothing then can be impossible, not even a miracle. For, as Scripture asks: "Can anything be too wonderful for God?"

Religious Jews, it should be clear by now, run a wide gamut in their evaluation of prayer.

It remains to be pointed out that, while the rule is not absolute, most traditionalists are maximalists, most modernists minimalists.

## 5. THE DAILY REGIMEN

This is the normal Jewish day as blocked out by the Tradition and practiced by all Jews in the past and by orthodox Jews to the present. In the main, this regimen is prescribed, being a matter of ritual law. But some of it represents folk-practice or local custom or individual option; all of it, including the legalistically determined elements, is subject in some degree to diversity of interpretation. So, within a framework of uniformity, a fair measure of variety and freedom is achieved.

On awakening and before he so much as stirs, a Jew thinks of his gratitude to God for life and the return of consciousness. "I give thanks before Thee," he prays, "King living and eternal, that Thou hast mercifully restored my soul to me; great is Thy faithfulness."

Then he rises, and with each act in the process of getting up recites an ordained blessing: on washing his hands and face, prescribed as his first duty; on setting foot on the ground; on attending to his bodily needs; on donning an undergarment adorned with the fringes commanded by the Torah. So he refers his every move to God and fulfills the instruction that a man shall be strong as a lion and fleet as a deer to do the will of his Father who is in Heaven. *

Then he prepares for formal worship. Again he wraps

* That the obligations of Jewish observance devolve more fully on males than females is due in part to the fact that Judaism had its beginnings in the Orient. It represents also a deliberate policy of the rabbis who, solicitous over woman's role as a home-maker, exempted her from "all positive precepts [as opposed to prohibitions] in which time constitutes a determining factor." In other words, she is relieved of all clock-bound commitments likely to interfere with her role as wife and mother.

himself in a fringed garment, save that this time it is the large, outer prayer-shawl worn only during religious exercises or sacred study. Next he takes up his *tefilin*, two little boxes encasing selected passages from Scripture, and, by means of the leather thongs with which they are equipped, ties them to himself, so fulfilling in utmost literalness the Biblical commandment: "Thou shalt bind them [i.e., God's words] for a sign upon thine hand, and they shall be for frontlets between thine eyes." One of these containers he fastens to his left arm, next to his heart; a symbolic commitment of heart and hand to God's will. The other he affixes to his forehead above his eyes, making a like consecration of his intellect. Finally he ties the leather thong about his left hand in a mystical knot suggestive of the divine name. With each act he recites apposite benedictions. With the last act, moreover, the entwining of the fingers, he pledges himself to God with Hosea's magnificent lines of spiritual espousal:

I will betroth thee unto Me forever;
Yea, I will betroth thee unto Me in righteousness, and in justice,
And in loving kindness, and in compassion.
And I will betroth thee unto Me in faithfulness;
And thou shalt know the Lord.

So, bound to God, wedded to His will, the Jew is ready for his morning devotions which consist in the recitation of Psalms; in prayers, some of personal reference, others affirming the group faith and ideals of Israel; and in passages from Scripture and rabbinic literature included for purposes of religious study.

The Tradition prefers that this order of worship be performed in a synagogue and with a congregation, though it accepts it when executed in private. Whether in one place or the other, it is not brief; as printed in one of the popular editions of the traditional prayerbook, it runs to almost ninety pages and may take as much as an hour to complete.

Not until it is finished and the *tefilin* have been doffed may a Jew partake of food. Ritual, however, continues, attending the breakfast and for that matter all other meals. Hands are washed and a brief benediction is spoken before bread is broken; a longer grace follows the repast. What is more, observances persist thereafter. Twice more, once in the afternoon and once again at dusk, the Jew engages in formal worship. Between times he invokes God's name frequently, since the Tradition ordains benedictions for almost every juncture of his life. Should he partake of food between meals, should he don a new garment, taste a fruit just then in season, see a flash of lightning, hear thunder, catch a glimpse of the ocean or of a rainbow or of trees burgeoning in the spring, encounter one learned in Torah or in secular lore, hear good news or be the recipient of bad—for almost every conceivable contingency there exists a brief but appropriate word of blessing. Furthermore, it is expected that he shall dedicate some period of each day to the study of the Tradition, either by himself or as a member of a class.

And at night on retiring he prays still again in gratitude for sleep, in reaffirmation of his faith, and in self-commitment to divine care; so that the day ends as it began, with the consciousness of God.

One wonders, perhaps, what time remains for work and play. Less, of course, than is available to a person who engages in fewer religious activities or none at all. But more than one would suppose. Most of the observances we have described are performed concurrently with the acts they mark and take no time whatsoever; many others require only a fleeting moment. As for the rest, the Tradition is not perturbed. What, it asks, are the supreme themes of human existence? Are they not God and the good life? Can time, then, be better spent than in their cultivation?

## 6. "THESE YE MAY EAT . . ."

The Tradition which regulates so much of life controls diet as well. Under the ordinances of the Torah and the enactments of the rabbis, a devout Jew may not eat the following:

—The flesh of animals, such as the horse or pig, whose hooves are not cloven and which do not chew the cud;

—The hind quarters of permitted animals;

—Fish that lack fins and scales;

—Fowl which are unclean in being birds of prey;

—All creeping things and insects, except for certain types of locusts.

Furthermore, the acceptable beasts and fowl must be slaughtered in a prescribed manner and by a qualified person licensed to that purpose. They must reveal no evidences of serious disease, especially in the lungs. They must be drained of blood, a result effected first by the method of slaughter and second by soaking and salting meat before it is cooked.

Still again, meat and meat products may not be prepared, served, or eaten with milk or milk derivatives; nor may utensils and dishes belonging to one category be mixed with the other. What is more, a specified interval must elapse between partaking of meat and milk.

Anything edible by ritualistic standards is *kosher*, which means literally fit or suitable. Anything forbidden is denominated *terefah;* a word signifying originally a living thing that had fallen victim to a beast or bird of prey and hence unacceptable as a food, but subsequently extended to cover all unacceptable foods.

We shall discuss later the theory underlying Jewish observance in general. The Jewish dietary rules, however, loom so large in public notice, are so unusual—bizarre, some would say—that an advance and special examination seems to be called for.

To the Jewish traditionalist these practices are but one segment of a larger circle, the whole of which is underpinned by the single classic premise: that all of Judaism is divinely inspired. This first principle posited, there can be no difficulties with rules concerning food, which find their simple justification in the fact that God ordained them. Beyond this no further accounting is required, and there are traditionalists who refuse to offer any.

Most traditionalists, however, while standing no less firmly on the doctrine of revelation, are ready to speculate as to whys and wherefores. Concerning the dietary code they point out:

1. It is in no slight part hygienic in purpose. Witness its concern over the healthiness of slaughtered animals, most particularly its ordinance that their lungs be examined scrupulously for symptoms of tuberculosis. This same motivation, it is suggested, may lie behind the rejection of swine's meat and shellfish as articles of food; the former because it is derived from an uncleanly creature which is furthermore a

carrier of trichinosis, the latter because it deteriorates rapidly and dangerously. *

2. It is, in further part, humanitarian. Hence the extraordinary requirement for a licensed slaughterer: that he shall be a devout and educated person; on the assumption that, being such, he will prove the more merciful in his occupation and less susceptible to brutalization by it. Hence too the careful specifications of the Tradition concerning the process of slaughter, to the detail that the knife used shall be razor-keen and free from notches so that its incision may be as nearly painless as possible.

3. It embodies vestiges of Judaism's struggle against idolatry in ancient times. Some of the dietary practices now prohibited were once associated with pagan cults and were banned originally for that reason, the interdict surviving, as so often in social patterns, the conditions that evoked it.

4. It is a spiritual discipline and has value as such. Practicing it, the Jew is schooled in the first lesson of the moral life: to say *no* to himself. Whereby he is fortified for larger and more difficult self-negations.

5. It has high survival-value for the Jewish group, serving as a reminder to Jews of their identity and as a deterrent to their being swallowed up by the non-Jewish world. Judaism, like all minority faiths, stands constantly in the peril of being

---

* Historic Judaism has always laid heavy stress on cleanliness. We have already noted its insistence on the washing of hands before the breaking of bread. The hygienic design in the dietary laws may well be another case in point. The Tradition provides further for the establishment of public ritual bath houses in every community and specifies the times and occasions at which they are to be visited.

This preoccupation with cleanliness stands forth the more remarkably when it is contrasted with the attitude widespread in the Middle Ages whereunder dirt was not only acquiesced in but was sometimes regarded as a concomitant of saintliness.

absorbed unto oblivion. Only on a foundation of preservative group practices can it persevere in its higher aims.

These are the considerations with which the traditionalist may further justify a system of practices which, in his eyes, is already justified superabundantly by the will of God as made known through revelation.

Modernists range in their attitudes and behavior concerning the dietary code all the way from total disapproval and nonobservance to complete assent and adherence.

Some insist that the regimen is no longer a proper part of the Jewish religion. Rejecting the doctrine of literal inspiration, they are so far from sharing the traditionalist's great first premise that they look for the origins of the Jewish diet not in divine omniscience but in the folkways of ancient men. Nor are they persuaded by the other arguments from hygiene, humanitarianism, and the rest. They will concede that the system may have been useful enough in the past; they hold that with changing circumstances its worth has diminished to the vanishing point.

Many modernists, perhaps most, are less radical. To be sure, they too do not base their advocacy of the code on any theory of revelation. Yet they see other values in it—all those we have already listed—plus one more. The dietary regimen is to them part of the age-old pattern of deportment of the House of Israel. As faithful members of that House they seek to conform to its rules even when these rules appear arbitrary, much as a gentleman defers to the domestic traditions of the home in which he is a guest, or all of us to conventional etiquette.

In matters of diet, then, religious Jews exhibit every conceivable degree of performance and nonperformance. And every imaginable paradox as well. For it is not unknown that a very devout Jew—devout in the sense that he is constantly and keenly aware of God—may eat ham with an untroubled conscience, whereas his fellow who admits to no theology at all may abstain from forbidden foods out of respect for the historic practices of his people or in assertion of his oneness with it.

## 7. THE SACRED ROUND

These are the festivals and the holy days ordained by the Tradition:

—The *Sabbath*, memorial of creation and of the exodus from Egypt; day of rest for man and beast, for bond and free alike; on which all labor, striving and anxiety are put away, so that man may enjoy—to use a piquant phrase of the ancient rabbis—a foretaste of the better world to come. The first institution in all history answering to the human need for a regularly recurrent day of release and refreshment, no less admirable in its recognition of the universality of that need, it ranks among the foremost contributions of the Hebraic spirit to personal happiness and social welfare.

Whatever the case with the Sabbath in other religions, there is not the least suggestion of "blueness" about it in its original, Jewish incarnation. On the contrary it is very much a day of joy and lightness of heart. In the synagogue it is marked by hymns and elaborated worship; in the home by the donning of one's best and gayest clothes, by the kindling of candles at its inception in the sunset hours, by the *Kiddush*, an inaugural prayer of benediction intoned over a wine cup, by festive meals and table songs, by relaxation, conversation, and informal study, and at its very conclusion by the

*Havdalah,* a picturesque ceremonial of division wherein the gladsome and sacred day is sent away with the savor of wine, the fragrance of sweet spices, and the light of a candle.

Beautiful in itself, the beauty of the Jewish Sabbath has been enhanced by a rich embroidery of folklore; its envisagement, for example, as a fair and chaste bride descending on the rays of the setting sun to her faithful one; the legend of the two angels who accompany each householder on its eve as he wends his way homeward from the synagogue; the conception that for its duration every devout Jew is possessed of an additional soul—an extra measure, so to speak, of spirituality; and all the other poetic notions, quaint or majestic, romantic or edifying, with which the myth-making capacity of a highly imaginative people could envelop a deeply loved institution.

A delight and medicament to the observant Jew, the Sabbath is also something more; it has ever been a restorative of the vigor of Judaism and the Jewish group—so potent a restorative that there is literal validity to the epigram of Ahad HaAm, modern philosopher of Judaism: "More than Israel has kept the Sabbath, the Sabbath has kept Israel."

—The *New Year, Rosh Hashanah;* marking, as its name indicates, the inauguration of a new year, the anniversary according to legend of the world's creation; and, appropriately enough, the occasion set aside by the Tradition for the reaffirmation of the sovereignty of God and for the quest after the regeneration of the heart.

—*Yom Kippur,* the *Day of Atonement,* a solemn white fast, during which from dusk to dusk the faithful partake of neither food nor drink in token of penitence, but through prayer and confession scrutinize their lives, abjure their evil-doing, and seek regeneration, a returning to God and goodness.

—*Tabernacles, Sukkoth;* a happy round of nine days the first eight of which celebrate the completion of the harvest, the dwelling of the ancient Israelites in booths in the desert, and the never interrupted sojourn of man under God's sheltering wings; the last of which, *Simhath Torah*, the *Rejoicing in the Torah*, marks the completion and rebeginning in the synagogue of the annual cycle of the reading of the Torah-Book.

—The *Passover, Pesah;* bearing a twofold reminder of the advent of the springtide and of the liberation of Israel from Egypt, and bright with promise of the deliverance which in the future awaits Israel and all mankind.

—*Pentecost, Shavuoth;* part agricultural festival in that it is the time of the grain harvest and of the in-bringing of the first fruits, and part historic-moral holiday in that it commemorates the revelation at Sinai.

—*Hanukkah*, the *Festival of Lights*, in recollection of the victory won by the Maccabees of old in the cause of freedom of conscience, and so a symbol of the uncoercibility of the human spirit.

—*Purim*, the *Day of Lots*, in which Israel relives its deliverance from the hands of Haman and takes renewed faith in its ability to outlive the Hamans of other times.

—*Tish'a B'Ab*, the *Ninth day of the Month of Ab*, the black fast; spent in mourning for the destruction of the first and second Temples in Jerusalem.

—And lesser fasts and lesser festivals: the days of *New Moon*, the *Seventeenth of Tammuz*, the *Ten Days of Penitence*, the *Thirty-third Day of the Omer*. . . .

So the year is adorned with many colors and much poetry:

rams' horns sounding alarms to lethargic souls; white robes on the scrolls of the Torah in symbol of purity and rebirth; palm branches and citrons; wide-branching eight-armed candelabra illumined each night with increasing light; noisemakers drowning out a persecutor's name; doors being opened for Elijah, forerunner of the delivering Messiah; the sad intonation of the Book of Lamentations; the seven prophetic lessons of consolation; the eerie midnight service which inaugurates the season of penitence. . . .

So too is the year transmuted into a round of sacred occasions gay and austere reflecting Israel's past, man's timeless aspirations, and the hopes of both for the future.

### 8. THE LIFE CYCLE

Most of living is sameness and recurrence. But some of it is uniqueness; there are occasions that come once, never to be repeated.

For the latter as for the former the Tradition has made provision, touching, whether with prescription or voluntary act, whether with fixed or elastic liturgy, every high moment and crucial juncture.

Rites attend birth:

—The circumcision of male children whereby the covenant between God and Israel is sealed into the very flesh of the infant Israelite;

—The naming of babies—boys at the circumcision, girls in the synagogue in an invocation recited during the reading of the Torah;

—The redemption of the first born, imaging forth the parents' awareness that their child is a trust with which God has invested them.

Rites cluster about turning points in the lives of children:

—The beginning of their religious education:

—The *Bar Mitzvah* ceremonial for boys, occurring as they enter adolescence, thus at an appropriate time for the assumption of the obligations of the Tradition;

—The analogous *Confirmation*, or *Bas Mitzvah*, for girls; a form of service instituted in modernist synagogues during the last century.

Rites adorn and sanctify wedlock:

—The solemnizing of the betrothal;

—The calling of the groom to the reading of the Torah in the synagogue on the Sabbath before his marriage;

—The marriage service itself, mellow with time and rich in gracious symbolisms: the canopy under which groom and bride stand side by side as in their new household; the wine cup from which they drink together; the ring and the ancient formula wherewith the man takes the woman to wife; the seven benedictions recited by the officiant in praise of God and in gratitude for the happiness of the event; the wine glass shattered in representation of sorrow amidst joy, sorrow for the broken House of Israel and the afflictions of all mankind; and the exclamation thereupon of *Mazal Tov*, invoking good fortune upon the newlyweds;

—The dedication of a new home and the affixing onto its door-posts of the *Mezuzah* prescribed by the Torah so that those who dwell there may ever be reminded of God's will.

Rites hallow death and mourning:

—Confession at death's door and self-commitment to God's mercy, followed by the ultimate and climactic proclamation of faith;

—The rending of garment in token of bereavement;

—The kindling of the memorial candle which continues to burn as does the soul which is, says Proverbs, the very lamp of God;

—The bathing of the body;

—The simple white shroud and unadorned and inexpensive coffin to which the body is consigned so that even as death comes to all equally, all may be equal in it;

—The rituals of the funeral and interment, reaching their dénouement in the mourner's first recitation of the *Kaddish* wherein he sanctifies God's name and accepts His will;

—The first week of sorrow when the grieving one sits aloof from his normal concerns, and his comforters make of his household their place of worship;

—The eleven months during which he says the *Kaddish* prayer;

—The tombstone set at the end of a year;

—The *Yahrzeit*, the annual commemoration, through the kindling of a candle and the recitation of the *Kaddish*, of the dead and the day of death;

—The *Yizkor* service on the Day of Atonement, Passover, Pentecost and Tabernacles, wherein all the living recall all their departed ones.

In these many fashions the Tradition attends the Jew in the climactic experiences of his life, endowing his every significant moment with the added significance of faith and idealism, adorning each exalted hour with befitting poetry joyous or solemn as may be required, tying his life cycle to Judaism and so investing it with an elevation and duration beyond itself.

## 9. WHYS AND WHEREFORE

To the traditionalist, as we have so often pointed out by now, the final reason for Jewish observance is the axiom of revelation. And that not only in the case of practices specifically prescribed in the Torah-Book or traceable to it, but also with those which are optional or merely customary. For, the latter tie in with the former and ultimately depend on them.

Given this postulate, no further argument is required. Accordingly, an ancient rabbi, called upon to justify an especially baffling ritual ordained by the Torah, responded in all simplicity and confidence: "Thus says God, 'I have issued a statute and enacted a decree; and ye are not at liberty to deviate from it.'"

Indeed, from time to time in Jewish history theological purists protested against all efforts at "seeking out reasons for the commandments." The fact of revelation, they insisted, was self-sufficient, needing no supplementation by human conjecture. Besides, they contended, to base a ceremonial on a man-made theory was to put it in jeopardy. Suppose the theory was not too well constructed or, having convinced one generation, failed to persuade another. Would not the effect be to encourage throwing out the usage with the justification?

In rigid logic, such purists were obviously right. And yet the quest for explanations never ceased, even among the most traditionalist of traditionalists.

Why? In part because the human mind hungers insatiably for understanding. Not content to be assured that God must have His reasons for His ordinances, it wants to know what these may be. In part, no doubt, because some observances are so clear as to intention that men cannot refrain from drawing obvious inferences. Contrariwise, other forms are so obscure that no one can resist speculating about them.

Whatever the motives, rationalizations of Jewish observance over and beyond the hypothesis of revelation have been advanced in the past and are being put forth nowadays as well. Among these the following are the most consequential:

1. Judaism as a way of life.

Judaism, being more than a church, is broader in its interests than theology and ethic. It is, in fact, no less than a full way of life. Wherefore it seeks to mold not only the beliefs, morals, and worship of the Jew, but his every act, his eating, drinking, work, and play. Ritual is the instrument designed to this end, carrying the Jewish religion into every nook and cranny of his being until nothing he does is untouched by Judaism.

2. The Sanctification of Life.

A key objective of Judaism, as we have already observed, is the sanctification of life. Every moment, the Tradition contends, ought to be suffused with the awareness of God and with moral fervor. To this end each turn of man's existence should be accompanied by acts evocative of religious and ethical idealism. Under this conception, Jewish ritual is intended as a spiritualizing device, a kind of persistent and all-pervading whispering of the verse in Numbers: "and ye shall look upon this and remember all the commandments of the Lord."

3. Ritual as Discipline.

In connection with the dietary laws, we registered the proposition that they discharge a disciplinary function, constituting a whetstone on which the will sharpens its cutting edge. This utility has long been ascribed to the whole system of observance. "The prime purpose of the commandments," said an ancient rabbi, "is to purify human nature."

Ritual is seen as a form of training in another, more general sense.

Religion like everything else has to be tended if it is to matter. Regular seasons must be set aside for it, as for any other serious interest, and during these times prescribed exercises must be performed.

A musician must practice by prearranged schedule, regardless of his inclination at the moment. So with the devout soul. It may not rely on caprice or put its hope in chance. It must work. The man on the other hand who folds his hands, waiting for the spirit to move him to think of God—who postpones worship for the right mood and the perfect setting, a forest or mountain peak, for example—will do little of meditating or praying. After all, how often does one find himself in a "cathedral of nature," and when by infrequent chance he does who shall say that he will be in a worshipful temper?

The effectively pious man then is very likely to be none other than the one who toils over his religion according to a program of specified acts at stated hours.

4. Ritual as Pedagogy.

Observance is a form of instruction and one of extraordinary effectiveness. It educates not on random occasions but constantly. It employs the sound technique of teaching by action rather than with words. It deals not in abstractions but in their tangible expression. It operates everywhere, as much in the home as in the synagogue, and in the market place, too. It is understood by all: the child and adult, the naive and the sophisticated. All in all, it may well be religion's best single instrument of indoctrination.

5. Ritual as Participation in the Historic.

He who adheres to a communion cannot but be aware that he is continuing a past and anticipating a future. In that consciousness is romance, the drama of being bound up with persons and occasions long gone or yet to be. The individual is lifted out of his particular time, place, and self into an enlargement of perspective and experience. His private and insular destiny is joined with the human mainland.

But it is not enough, if a man is to derive all this from his religion, for him to think and feel at one with it. He must engage in its practices also.

To specify: a Jew will feel most thoroughly identified with the career of his people and faith when he observes the Sabbath, celebrates the Passover feast, or stands in the presence of the Torah scroll; that is, on the occasions when his hand as well as his head and heart is busy with the gestures which in their generations his forefathers executed and which in time to come will be performed by his descendants also.

6. Ritual as Fellowship.

By the same token, a man's solidarity with his fellows is firmest when he and they act together and alike. Never is a Jew surer of himself as a Jew than in the hours when all Jews everywhere engage in identical ritual acts—on Passover Eve, for example, or on the Day of Atonement. What is more, he will tend to be stronger in his own convictions for the knowledge that he does not stand alone in either faith or its expression, but that those like-minded with him make up a numerous and distinguished company.

7. Ritual as an Aesthetic.

What poetry and music are to language, that ritual is to

conduct. Onto the hardheadedness and practicality of existence it throws a splash of color and passion. Candles are lit,
spice boxes are sniffed, rams' horns blown, liturgies intoned;
a past revived, an unborn future anticipated. This, not the
prose of living, affords a man many of his softest, dearest
memories and evokes from him emotions not otherwise to be
duplicated. In a word, ritual is one of the arts whose cultivation lends beauty to living.

8. Ritual as Survival Mechanism.

A minority communion everywhere, Judaism is exposed
to the corrosives of other faiths and cultures. Against ever-
threatened dissolution, ritual serves as a shell, enfolding and
protecting tender inner parts and the spirit that informs them.

Dangers inhere in the device. Ceremonials may come to
be ends in themselves, prized without regard to the values
they shield. Or they may hypertrophy, growing thick to the
point of immobilizing, even suffocating the life process they
contain.

Against these diseases no religion is immune. With its highly
developed ritual apparatus, Judaism may well be peculiarly
susceptible to them. As a whole, however, the Tradition has
fought off the threat. In any case it is a peril that must be
risked. For it is questionable whether stripped of protective
armor Judaism could long endure.

### 10. MODERNIST VARIATIONS ON THE RITUAL THEME

The traditionalist's postscript is the modernist's entire
epistle.

The former begins his rationale of ritual with revelation
and may or may not supplement it with other contentions.
The latter has only the "other considerations" to advance.

This divergence in thought leads inevitably to some divergence in action. Traditionalists and modernists quite often practice diversely or, if similarly, with different moods and intents. Of the distinctions between the two groups four are of largest moment.

First, the traditionalist insists on maintaining the ancestral pattern intact. Since for him it embodies God's will, he will, except where the Tradition itself explicitly permits, not presume to play the eclectic or innovator with it.

The modernist on the other hand may assay either role. In his view the Jewish regimen is a human device—not without a divine impulsion—but still human and hence always subject to improvement.

Wherefore the modernist dares to articulate questions which the traditionalist will not so much as contemplate. Why did a particular ritual come into being to begin with? What purpose did it fulfill then? Does it serve any worthwhile end nowadays? Could it do its job more effectively were it modified? Or has it so lost relevance and effectiveness that it may just as well be dropped altogether?

Now it must not be supposed that the modernist looks only to his own reason and experience for answers to these queries. Modernist though he be, he is a traditionalist also, reverent of the past and partial to it. All things being equal he is inclined to decide in its favor. In sum, he tries always to operate within the Tradition or, if beyond it, at least in its general neighborhood.

Second, traditionalists are uniform, modernists diverse in their observance.

The former follow the standard historic code; the latter diverge from it in all directions and degrees.

Third, the emotional texture of observance varies from

group to group, even when one and the same rite is being performed by both.

The traditionalist is marked by a scrupulousness of spirit, a seriousness—almost an anxiety—over rituals, sometimes over their minutiae. Of God's ordaining, he feels they deserve his utmost concern.

The modernist is more casual and relaxed. Rites in his eyes are usages, means to ends. They merit respect, but only as a conscientious workman respects his important tools.

Fourth, the modernist is not only ready to change the old if necessary, he is eager for the new. He wants each age to evolve innovations. So, he believes, the common store will grow ever richer with time.

The traditionalist is almost as wary of additions to the Tradition as of subtractions. In illustration of this distrust the eighteenth century folk preacher, Jacob Kranz of Dubno, wove a shrewd homily. Taking as his text the Torah verse: "Thou shalt not add thereto [i.e., God's ordinance] nor diminish from it," the lecturer inquired with what logic the Torah might object to adding to its commandments? If one Day of Atonement a year be spiritually salutary, why is a person enjoined against undertaking to observe two?

Which question the homilist answered with a parable. A man, he said, once borrowed his neighbor's silver candlesticks. Promptly at the time stipulated he returned them together with a little candlestick which, he related, had been born to the originals and therefore properly accompanied them.

Now, the owner knew full well that candlesticks do not procreate. Before him, however, lay a windfall. And so, not disputing his neighbor's tale, he accepted his own property and its supposed increase.

The next week, another borrowing—this time of silver forks—and another restoring, again with progeny. In this fashion, incident followed incident, the lender congratulating himself with mounting fervor on his inexplicable good fortune.

Then came a day when the borrower asked for all his neighbor's silver at once, parents and children alike. This time, however, nothing at all was repaid. Neither the loan nor increment. For, as the borrower solemnly informed the owner, a plague had broken out in silverware; the candlesticks, the forks, the goblets, and so on, had all died. And indeed, if metallic objects can have children, certainly it must be assumed of them that they are liable to mortality.

So, said Jacob of Dubno, the danger of adding to Jewish usage lies not in the adding, but in the fact that he who has once accustomed himself to be free with additions will in the end take liberties as to subtractions.

A Judaism constant versus a Judaism evolving, this emerges as the fundamental issue between traditionalists and modernists on observance as on so much else in the Jewish religion.

# VIII

## 1. LAW IN JUDAISM

Is not law in Judaism much like Saul among the prophets, that is to say, distinctly out of place? What, after all, can a system of jurisprudence be doing in the company of a faith, an ethic, and a ritual?

And yet the Jewish religion contains a body of law, not only ecclesiastical, which would be readily understandable, but civil and criminal also.

What is more, law in Judaism is not some half-forgotten detail tucked away in a corner. Quite the contrary, it stands out in the open, looming large. It is the theme of an extensive literature, including some of the greatest texts of the Tradition; it was the first interest of many of the most brilliant minds and noblest spirits among medieval Jews; it is widely studied and cultivated to this day.

And all this despite the fact that much of it has long been purely academic. Whole areas of it have never been intended for application beyond the borders of Palestine. Other sections deal with or presuppose a Temple at Jerusalem, nonexistent these nineteen centuries. And still other portions—the corpus of criminal law, for example—have been supplanted by the codes of the lands in which Jews live. Indeed, of the Six Orders into which, after the precedent of the

*Mishnah*, Jewish law is customarily divided, only two are throughout of pragmatic consequence: the Order *Moed*, Religious Festivals; and *Nashim*, Domestic Relations, with two more pertinent in part.

A paradox, a nest of paradoxes, that a legal system should be included in a religion to begin with, and then that it should be the object of so much attention when so little of it can be practiced.

Yet the riddle is not hard to unravel.

Law is present in Judaism first of all because it is present in the Torah-Book. Of and by itself this circumstance suffices to make it a permanent element in the Tradition.

Law is part of Judaism in the second place because the Jews are more than members in a religious communion, being also fellows in a historic people. For about a millennium and a half that people lived its own life on its own soil and in conformity with its own political and moral principles. Quite understandably, it amassed in the process a sizable body of juridical materials.

What is more, even after the dispersal of the Jews they continued in greater or lesser measure to regulate themselves by their national code. All through the Middle Ages down to the nineteenth century Jewish communities were autonomous, at least in internal affairs. To be sure, there had been written into the Tradition the dictum of Mar Samuel, distinguished legal scholar of the third century, to the effect that the civil law of the land, so long as it was consistent with essential Judaism, was to be regarded by Jews as binding on themselves. Nevertheless, Jews commonly preferred their own courts for the settlement of disputes. Which means that as recently as a century ago Jewish law still functioned as a social instrument.

Also, law persists in the Tradition because the study of

it, like any other mental occupation, can be pleasurable, as many Jews in each generation have discovered to their delight. To this purpose it does not matter in the least whether the subject matter is or is not operative. It may still pique men's curiosity and elicit from them the resolve toward understanding and mastery. It becomes a pure science, a pursuit engaged in not for tangible advantage but for intellectual joy. Always there has been something of this spirit in the study of Jewish law, a temper made all the keener because all through the Middle Ages the world allowed Jews so few other outlets for their energies.

Law is an element in Judaism, last of all, because of the intense Jewish preoccupation with ethics, and because of the historic Jewish insistence that ideals need to be put to work. If they be personal they must be translated into habits and disciplines. If they be social they must be incarnated in institutions, folkways, and law. Otherwise, their cogency and content will evaporate, and they will be left in the end empty vessels.

Persuaded of this truth, the Tradition has refused to permit its social values to go unapplied. Steadfastly, passionately, it has struggled for their utilization as guiding rules for the social process.

This then is the final and climactic reason for the presence of law in Judaism. It could not be otherwise, Judaism being what it is: a religion impelled by a vigorous social idealism and determined to put this idealism to use.

### 2. APPLIED IDEALISM

Characteristically enough, the Torah-Book, the earliest formulation of Jewish ideals, contains also their first implementation.

Is man made in the image of God? Then, to take illustrations at random, the stranger may not be oppressed; and the wages of a hired servant may not be withheld; and the slave girl shall be protected against abuse by her master; and no man shall bear the penalties of another's offenses; nor may a creditor enter a debtor's house to claim payment; the slaying of a slave is as much murder as the killing of a free man; and when the bondman goes free, his term of service concluded, he shall be well compensated by way of severance.

Are all men equal before God? Then there must be but one law for the Israelite and the stranger in his gates, and justice may not be perverted whether out of deference toward the rich or out of sympathy for the poor.

Are men brothers, owing one another fraternal solicitude? Then let a tithe be taken up for the indigent; the needy may lawfully claim for their own the corners of fields, the gleanings, and anything overlooked in the harvesting. Therefore, too, anyone who requires it may enter a field and eat, save that he may carry nothing away. Hence also the accepting of interest is prohibited, nor may a millstone or cloak be taken as security for a loan.

Are the world's goods a trust imparted by God to mankind? Then, loans shall be canceled every seventh year so that no one may forever be sunk in debt; and bondsman may not, except at his explicit request, be indentured for more than six years; nor may the land be sold in perpetuity but shall be returned every fifty years to the descendants of its original owners so that the impoverished may have fresh access to the soil from which they have been dispossessed.

The Biblical precedent of high ideals courageously applied carries over into post-Biblical Judaism. The *Mishnah* and the *Talmuds* are as passionate and determined to implement justice and mercy as were the prophets. In effect, the rabbis picked up where Scripture left off, enacting legislation extraordinary for humanity and liberalism.

First in human history, they challenged capital punishment, virtually abolishing it in their courts.

They guarded the person and rights of the slave; in fact they all but did away with Hebrew slavery.

They guaranteed the right to strike.

They established a legal presumption in favor of labor in disputes between workers and their employers.

They instituted universal compulsory education.

Orientals though they were, they protected zealously the rights of women and improved their status.

They worked out the first systematic philanthropy in human history.

But what of the crucial issues of our day?

Where does Judaism stand on these? Which of the conflicting ideologies, what specific social reforms does it endorse?

To these questions there can be no detailed answers. The prophets and rabbis who were the chief architects of the Tradition lived in an age other than ours when ideologies such as the democratic, totalitarian, capitalist, socialist, and communist had not yet been conceived, and when our social dilemmas did not exist, at least not in their present form.

Yet the Tradition is so clear in its basic social outlook that deductions can with confidence be drawn from it for contemporary problems. These deductions, like all inferences, carry with them some element of risk. And they take the form not of specific conclusions, but of general principles.

But the risk is not so great nor the principles so abstract as to deprive the Tradition of social relevance. On the contrary, a fairly compact outlook can be extracted from it readily and with high assurance, as is attested by the pronouncements in recent years of the various rabbinical bodies. These associations are separated by all sorts of theological and ritualistic chasms, yet each of them has promulgated a quite concrete social program, and all the programs coincide on all important themes, clear evidence that the Tradition is still capable of investing Jewish social thought with unity and particularity.

On the evidences of the past and of the modern rabbinate, Judaism stands these days:

—For the fullest freedom, political, economic, and social, for every individual and group, which includes among other things, maximal civil liberties, trade unionism, the equality of all;

—For the social use of wealth, though whether this involves social *ownership* and if so to what extent is disputed among contemporary interpreters of Judaism;

—For a society based on co-operation as its root rule rather than competition;

—For international peace guaranteed by a world government, the notion of the absolute sovereignty of the national state having always been an obscenity in the eyes of the Tradition.

What does all this add up to in the prevailing parlance?

Quite clearly to political democracy, to a modification of capitalism in the direction of economic democracy, and to a world state.

This sum total is not as exact as might be desired, but neither is it so vague as to be mistakable.

### 3. THE TWO VIEWPOINTS

To traditionalists Jewish law possesses all the authority, prestige, and worth of the rest of Judaism. It is something to be studied at all times, to be practiced now so far as circumstances permit, and destined, in the future Messianic age when Israel has been restored to its ancient land, to be exercised again in its fullness.

Modernists divide, in their attitude to Jewish law, into two groups: a right wing made up of those closer to the traditionalist outlook, and a left composed of those further removed from it.

The more conservative group wishes to keep the more relevant sections of Jewish Law operative; those, for example, regulating domestic affairs, festival observances, and ritual forms. Furthermore, if they are Zionists they may hope for the revitalization of the Jewish legal heritage in the Homeland now being established in Palestine.

The radicals contend that, whatever its worth in the past, law no longer belongs in Judaism, nor for that matter in any religion as modern men understand religion. The regulation of human affairs by judicial processes pertains to the state and not to the church or synagogue. It is the business of the various communions to inspire men with ideals; their implementation should be left to political arms.

But even the most left-wing of modernists, though he has no desire to apply Jewish law, agrees with the most ardent traditionalist in seeing value in the study of it.

It is a sure clue to Judaism's social ethic and more trustworthy than any other, since religions like men reveal their characters in the things they work hardest for. And it projects into prominence a thesis too often neglected, that the ideal has reality only if realized.

# IX

INSTITUTIONS

## I. THE SYNAGOGUE

Whatever spot Jews set aside for their religious exercises, wherever they put up an Ark containing the Torah-scroll, source and symbol of the Tradition, there is a synagogue. No dedicatory rites or sacramental procedures are required to hallow the place. The Tradition insists that the synagogue be cleanly; it urges that it be beautiful. Yet many a synagogue is little more than a bare room and is not a whit diminished in holiness on that account. For, it is the Jewish teaching concerning God that, since He is present everywhere, He may everywhere be invoked.

Three functions pertain to the synagogue:

—It serves as a "house of prayer," the sanctuary where public worship is conducted; the place, too, to which men may repair for their individual meditations and prayers;

—It is a "house of study," a school of Judaism, offering Jewish instruction to child and adult alike; or, if not itself the school, then its parent and stay;

—It is the "house of the people," where Jews may seek out other Jews, and through association with like-minded persons be strengthened in their loyalties.

A synagogue is not only a place but also the people who resort to it; that is to say, a congregation.

Any group of Jews may constitute themselves a congregation. Common sense indicates that congregations ought not to be multiplied needlessly. And none should be launched without fair assurance of the ability to muster a *minyan*, the quorum of ten males set by the Tradition as a prerequisite for formal worship. These conditions aside, Judaism sets no restrictions on establishing congregations.

Every congregation is altogether autonomous, free to choose its rabbi and other functionaries and to determine policies, large or small. It will, of course, be guided by the Tradition; but it will also decide for itself how the Tradition is to be construed and the extent to which it is to be followed. No institutional authority exists to which individual synagogues must render obedience. Congregations do co-operate with one another in *ad hoc* organizations established for specific and limited purposes and through permanent federations based on likemindedness of viewpoint and program. But all these are voluntary associations, capable of making recommendations to their constituents but without the least power to exact compliance.

But since the congregation itself is composed of persons who have come together of their own volition, reserving to themselves the right to continue, terminate, or transfer membership as they see fit, the final seat of authority in Jewish religious organizations is lodged in the individual and his conscience.

The freedom which modern Judaism accords to persons and congregations was not always as broad as it is today. Until the eleventh century there was always some seat of religious authority to which all the Jewries of the world deferred. And up to the last hundred and fifty years or so every local Jewish community was very tightly organized, though almost always on a democratic basis. A board of overseers, elected usually each year by the ballot of all Jewish householders, regulated all communal business. It might very well forbid the establishment of a new synagogue which it regarded as superfluous or schismatic; or discipline an individual or faction dangerous, in its opinion, to the general welfare or the continuity of the Tradition.

Not usually was such a local board or the central authority, when it existed, able to employ physical coercion to enforce its will. When challenged it could rely only on moral pressures. It could rebuke and censure; it could ostracize; in very grave cases it might resort to excommunication, suspending the recalcitrants from participation in the life of the community or expelling them from it permanently. Yet such normally was the *esprit de corps* of the Jewish group that though it lacked political arms the Jewish community maintained a high level of discipline.

The controls were there, yet, even under them, individuals and parties generally enjoyed considerable liberty. Unless there was a cogent reason to the contrary they were likely to be left free to form congregations as they desired and to follow the rabbis of their preference.

The latitude of the past has in our day expanded almost to infinity. In the total absence of central control, international, national, and local, each congregation, whether for better or worse, does pretty much what is right in its own eyes.

Liberty leads to diversity. Being free entities, congregations run the widest range of viewpoints and ritual modes. Through the variety, three major patterns can be traced:

—The Orthodox synagogue, in which the Tradition, full and unmodified, serves as sole and unquestioned authority on all matters of theology, practice, and liturgy. It is here that the Jewish past finds its contemporary embodiment. Observers can identify congregations of this stamp by several unmistakable signs: their total adherence to the historic prayerbook, the almost exclusive use of the Hebrew tongue in worship, the absence of instrumental music, the segregation of men and women during services, and the usage whereby the former pray with covered heads.

—The Conservative synagogue, representing right wing modernism, which seeks to abide by the Tradition so far as practicable; beyond that it yields to the more importunate demands of modern thought and life. The Tradition is tempered, recast, and reinterpreted on the one hand; on the other, the modifications are cautious, minimal concessions to *force majeure*. Worship accordingly bears marked resemblances to the Orthodox but also marked differences. The prayer text, for example, is quite traditional; the Hebrew language predominates; men furthermore cover their heads. Against that, some of the liturgy is recited in English, instrumental music may be employed, and men and women sit together.

—The Reform synagogue, or Temple, which embodies left modernism. Here the weight of the Tradition is least, the influence of contemporary thought and circumstance greatest. In consequence, reform worship is furthest removed from the historic pattern. It uses the English language in the main. Of the old rituals it retains only those it judges to be meaningful and congenial to the modern temper. It abandons altogether the covering of the head in prayer, the separation of men and women, and the ban against instrumental music.

The differences among Orthodox, Conservative, and Reform synagogues are in part the result of diversities of taste and, in further part, of divergent appraisals of the practical problems of Jewish living. But they cut much deeper. At work behind them also are conflicting theories of Judaism and clashing theological doctrines. Yet large and consequential as the dissimilarities may be their extent and significance should not be exaggerated.

Jews who stand very near the synagogue scene are especially prone to overestimate the number and importance of the cleavages which divide religious Jewry.

An Orthodox Jew in the heat of controversy may say of a Reform Temple that to him it is no more Jewish than a Quaker meeting house. Conversely, a Reform Jew may assert of Orthodox worship that, so far as he is concerned, it is as unintelligible and alien as a Greek Catholic service might be.

Neither means all he says. Certainly, no objective observer would confuse Reform Jewish worship with the Quaker, or Jewish Orthodoxy with Greek, or fail to see that the two Jewish sects are infinitely closer to each other than either is to any non-Jewish denomination.

Nor could it be otherwise, seeing that all designs for Jewish faith, liturgy, and rite are collateral descendants of an original pattern and that all regulate themselves consciously and are unconsciously molded by one and the same Tradition.

## 2. THE RABBINATE

Rabbis are teachers of the Tradition. They are generally called on to discharge additional functions as pastors, preachers, administrators, and communal leaders. But first and foremost they are teachers. This is the essence of their being.

To say of rabbis that they are teachers is to deny that they are priests. Unlike some other religions, Judaism does not assert of its clergy that they possess spiritual powers, conferred either by ordination or vocation, which are inaccessible to the laity. In its eyes no difference exists, except in training, between the man at the pulpit and those in the pews. Nor is there any rite at all which only the former can properly perform. Any layman who has the knowledge and the spiritual fitness may conduct worship and, if he has something to say and can get a congregation to listen to him, may preach.

Rabbis, further, are not "called," as some evangelical denominations understand the word. It is not required of them that they undergo a mystical experience of illumination or of selection by Providence for the ministry. They are, of course expected to enter the rabbinate in the spirit of self-consecration; to be good people, genuine as to belief and principle, ardently devoted to the Tradition and to the service of God, Israel, and mankind. But all these qualities Judaism hopes to find in every Jew; none of them belongs peculiarly to the rabbinate. In the end then the rabbi differs from his Jewish fellows only in being more learned than they, more expert in the Tradition they all share. He is a rabbi by virtue of education; his ordination is a graduation, his title an academic degree.

Until relatively recent times the learning required for the rabbinate was exclusively Hebraic, embracing Scripture, Talmudic literature, and the codes regulative of Jewish thought and practice. These subjects might be mastered in private study or by attendance at a *Yeshivah* or academy. To gain ordination, a candidate applied to some rabbi or rabbis of distinction, stood for examination both of character and knowledge of the Tradition, and, if he passed, was awarded a certificate entitling him to be called rabbi, to interpret Judaism, and to adjudicate matters of Jewish law. He was then eligible for a rabbinical post, to which any congregation might invite him, and concerning which he was a free agent as to acceptance.

Under this system, which was universal until the modern period and is still operative in Orthodox circles, many men qualified for ordination but never applied for it, being more concerned with learning than with diplomas and titles; many acquired ordination but did not seek rabbinical positions, preferring to remain laymen; and even those who undertook to serve congregations or communities often refused compensation. Indeed, all through ancient and medieval times Jewish clergymen and teachers were explicitly dissuaded by Jewish law from accepting salaries, on the ground that it was wrong and unseemly to exploit sacred learning to worldly advantage. Instead, the rabbi earned his livelihood like other men, as a farmer, artisan, or merchant, and ministered to his flock as a labor of love. Only in the later Middle Ages was this arrangement surrendered as no longer feasible.

The first duties of the traditionalist rabbi, past and present, are those of a chief scholar and judge. Of sermonizing he does very little, discourses in the synagogue being assigned normally to laymen who specialize in popular preaching. He is of course a guide to the perplexed, a pastor to the stricken, and a prime authority on communal matters. But his paramount functions are to pursue his own studies, to resolve scholarly problems for lay students, to sit as judge in disputes between Jews, and to resolve moot issues of ritual, observance, faith, and ethic—all, of course, in accordance with the Tradition.

It is worth recording that for at least the past thousand years the individual rabbi has enjoyed a high measure of intellectual and spiritual independence. Once all rabbis bowed to the authority of a supreme rabbinical court, the Sanhedrin. When that body dissolved—sometime in the fifth century—a portion of its power was conferred by unspoken consent upon the presidents and senates of two great Talmudical academies in Babylonia. In the eleventh century these too ceased to be effective forces. Thereafter no rabbi has owed obedience to any other, except in tribute to superior attainments. In theory at least, and generally in practice, each rabbi has been a free, autonomous spirit, deferring only to the Tradition and his own conscience.

The times have wrought their changes in the rabbinate.

It is no longer regarded as enough these days that a rabbi shall be learned in Jewish lore; a broad, secular education is required of him as well.

Training for the rabbinate has ceased to be as informal as it was once; and ordination by individual rabbis has all but disappeared, except among the strictest of traditionalists. Men prepare for the rabbinate and are ordained nowadays by seminaries.

Then, too, the rabbinate has become a profession from which its practitioners derive a livelihood.

The functions of rabbis have been modified sharply. Even in traditionalist circles, preaching, the supervision of religious education, and pastoral ministrations have tended to supplant scholarship and judicial duties as the first rabbinical charges. To which have been added in most instances the obligations of congregational administration, of communal causes, and, since Jews are no longer confined to Ghettos but participate in civic life, of general leadership as well.

Yet in three most vital respects rabbis today are expected to be what they always have been:

—It is assumed that they will be free agents, owing moral allegiance only to the Tradition and their own souls;

—It is expected that they shall be morally qualified for their calling;

—It is taken for granted that they are and ought to be primarily teachers of the Tradition. Modern living and its demands often work havoc with this time-honored criterion. But when Judaism is truest to itself it remains a living ideal. For, Judaism being what it is, what else shall rabbis be in the first instance if not those who know, and knowing, teach?

# WORLD-TO-COME

## X

## 1. THE TRIPLE HOPE

"There is hope for thy latter end," sang the prophet.

A hope threefold is in its reference.

The hope we have already described for the Jewish people: the expectation of its ultimate deliverance and vindication.

A hope also for the individual soul: the trust that it will not be swallowed up in death but, surviving the body, will in some fashion attain the fulfillment of which it falls short in the flesh.

A hope for society: the assurance that it will in the end be regenerated into something fairer, its evils purged away, its good perfected and made permanent.

Together these three make one mighty, joyous confidence: the confidence that for man, for Israel and for mankind a better time lies ahead than has ever yet been.

## 2. THE DESTINY OF MAN

Concerning the final outcome of man's career, the traditionalist affirms three doctrines: Recompense, Immortality, and Resurrection.

### Recompense

Judaism teaches that men should not serve God in the spirit of "bondsmen who tend their master for the sake of wages."

Yet it holds also that those who do the good deserve a reward. So the Tradition shares the demand of conscience that virtue be repaid and wickedness punished. As a whole and in the rough, life satisfies this requirement. Honesty usually brings security and esteem in its train. He who gives love is most likely to be the recipient of it.

Unfortunately, the exceptions to this rule are frequent and sometimes flagrant. Many a rogue has passed his days in ease and prosperity, many a saint in adversity and grief.

But God is a God of justice. If man does not meet with perfect equity during his lifetime, then, the Tradition insists, he will find it afterward. There, in the next world, the crooked will be made straight, and to each will be given according to his deserts.

### Immortality

Death cannot be and is not the end of life.

Man transcends death in many altogether naturalistic fashions. He may be immortal biologically, through his children; in thought, through the survival of his memory; in influence, by virtue of the continuance of his personality as a force among those who come after him; and ideally, through his identification with the timeless things of the spirit.

When Judaism speaks of immortality it has in mind all these. But its primary meaning is that man contains something independent of the flesh and surviving it; his consciousness and moral capacities, his essential personality: a soul.

This it is which transcends mortality and which, the Tradition holds, is recompensed in life after death.

As to the form of the hereafter, of the Paradise or Heaven or Eden where righteousness is said to be rewarded, of the

Hell or Sheol or Gehinnom where wickedness is punished—on this, as on so many other articles of belief, individual Jews have at all times put private interpretations. Indeed, it is questionable whether any other tenet of Judaism has been more divergently construed.

Heaven and Hell have been described by some as no more than states of the soul, by others as actual places, and by some of these in turn with elaborate details as to topography.

Conceptions of immortality have ranged from the highly abstract notion of a reabsorption of the soul into the Infinite to the most naive imaginings of the post-mundane continuance of earthly pursuits.

Man's deathlessness has been envisaged as involving the survival of the individual identity and awareness, and alternatively as impersonal and without consciousness.

The transmigration of the soul and its reincarnation have been affirmed by some and denied by others.

Here as elsewhere, and here more than anywhere else, the Tradition has allowed for latitude.

## Resurrection

But not even now, when man has been assigned to Heaven or Hell, is his destiny complete. There remains to be enacted one final, climactic episode.

On some day to come, the bodies of the dead of all time will arise from their graves, souls will be summoned from the places and states to which they have been committed, and both will be reunited as during their existence on earth.

Then on every human being, body and soul together, and in the presence of all the multitudes of all generations, God will pronounce judgment whether of bliss or damnation.

As with other doctrines, so with the Resurrection; variations in envisagement are quite permissible. The bodies of the resurrected have been conceived as transfigured, their corporeality etherialized into almost pure spirituality; they have been imagined as thoroughly physical. The duration of Resurrection has been supposed by some to be eternal, by others to be limited and destined to yield to another separation of body and soul, each returning to its everlasting estate.

Yet there are limits to the imaginative freedom permitted the individual. Under whatever form, the Tradition insists that a Jew shall hold to faith in Recompense, Immortality, and Resurrection. Nor may he believe in them as vague allegories. They must at the least mean for him something akin to what they seem to say.

No one, the Tradition holds, can accept less and still be a traditionalist Jew.

Jewish modernists accept less.

In the first place they differ from traditionalists even on the history of these articles of faith.

Traditionalists assume these doctrines to have been revealed at Sinai along with the whole body of Jewish conviction. They find them affirmed explicitly and by innuendo at various points in Scripture, including the earliest and most authoritative section, the Torah-Book.

Not so modernists. As they read the Bible, its most ancient portions have only this to say about an afterlife: that the souls of the dead are consigned to a shadowy underworld called *Sheol* where they continue in a vague and only partly conscious existence. The religion of even the great prophets, according to the modernist view, was without any suspicion of either Resurrection or Immortality as these came to be understood.

Only in the days of the Second Temple did these doctrines emerge, partly as a normal unfolding of potentialities latent in Judaism; partly in response to the stimulation of Zoroastrianism with its teachings concerning Resurrection and the Last Judgment, and of Hellenism with its highly developed notion of immortality.

On the basis of this historical construction, some few modernists draw the inference that neither Resurrection nor Immortality is integral to the Jewish religion. Judaism existed for long centuries without them; it can exist without them again.

Most modernists however would determine the present validity of these ideas not by history but by reason and experience.

Having tested traditional conceptions by these standards, they dismiss some and preserve others. They abandon the doctrines of the Resurrection of the body, at least in any literal sense; of an actual, spatial Heaven and Hell; and of eternal damnation.

They retain faith in the deathlessness of man's spirit not only in its naturalistic connotations but in its beyond-this-life significance as well. They are sparing of guesses as to what the state of immortality may be like but firm in the conviction that in some fashion the human personality outlives its corporeal housing.

Similarly they hold to the belief in Recompense, the trust that those who do the good somehow have good conferred on them, whereas those who devise evil, no matter what its form or object, work it also against themselves.

But as with Immortality so with Recompense. The proposition is affirmed without any guesses as to its attendant circumstances. No one claims to have detailed knowledge of the operations of God's justice.

Obviously, this whole complex of tenets has lost in substance among modernists. Yet elements of it survive, vigorous and potent. With their forefathers and their traditionalist contemporaries Jewish modernists continue to believe that though he die man lives on, and that the scales of cosmic equity always end up in balance.

### 3. THE KINGDOM OF GOD

Society even at its best is unworthy of man and unrepresentative of God.

Has there been, in all history, a single polity or economy which has revered man as he merits, God being his Father and Maker?

In what social order have the principles of justice, mercy, and mutual helpfulness been fittingly observed?

What community is there so good as to testify, not by words or speech but by deeds and institutions, to a God of goodness?

But the divine spark in man cannot forever be obscured. God's law must ultimately prevail and His nature finally assert itself in social affairs as everywhere else.

From which it follows that the present world order must in the end pass away, yielding to a new, free from the ancient evils of human history, consonant with the worth of every soul, conformable to the moral law, properly reflective of the God who stands behind the scheme of things.

To this perfected society of perfected men the Tradition gives the name: *Kingdom of God*.

God's Kingdom lies not in the future only. In outline

it is already at hand and perceptible. Do not stars and planets, seedlings and birds obey God's ordinance for them? Are they not even now His faithful subjects? And among men have there not been multitudes eager to know and serve Him, and even greater multitudes who, sporadically if not consistently, are of like heart? Is there not in the midst of the sinfulness of a wicked world much that is warm, sweet, right, and compassionate?

God's Kingdom is therefore more than a promise. Obscured and broken though it be, latent rather than overt, it is also an ever-present actuality. Everything in the world subserving goodness is of its dominion. Everyone ministering to the right is, whether knowingly or not, its citizen.

Touch Judaism where you will and you will come upon this concept of the Kingdom, this dream of a perfected world peopled by regenerated men.

Every benediction among the many ordained by the ancient rabbis refers to it explicitly.

Every formal service closes with a twofold prayer, in the first of which the worshiper offers obeisance to the Kingdom, in the second of which he prays for its speedy coming in its completeness.

The "Hear, O Israel" prayer, the classic confession of faith in Judaism, is interpreted by the rabbis as "the acceptance of the authority of the Kingdom."

The Kingdom is the theme too of the most solemn and exalted passage in the liturgy for the New Year Holy Day, which is itself one of the most solemn and exalted occasions in the Jewish calendar.

This heavy emphasis on the Kingdom becomes understandable when one considers that it embodies perhaps the most precious hope of the human spirit, and when one reflects further on its moral import, on the vast decisive implications with which it is fraught. For, given this conception, man's ethical life is remade. Above all other dreams this one stands supreme, above all other obligations the duties implicit in it: to be aware of the Kingdom, to advance it, to hasten the day of its "shining forth" over all the world and in the eyes of all men.

When the prophets first spoke of the Kingdom, they were introducing a notion radically new to man's imagination, such a vision as had never been seen before in all the ancient civilizations of the East, such an ideal as the classical cultures of the West were destined never to achieve for themselves. Beyond the sphere of Judaism men of antiquity had no hopes for the human future. They expected at best that what had been would be forevermore, if indeed they were not persuaded of the more melancholy notion that the world was running steadily downhill from a Golden Age distant in the past and forever irretrievable.

It was, then, a great revolution which Judaism effected with its good tidings of the Kingdom, a turning forward of the eyes, upward of the heart, onward of the feet; in sum, a reorientation of the total human being.

The revolution was all the greater because, with time, the hope of the Kingdom overflowed not only Judaism and the Jews but all churches and creeds, to become in the end the common property and inspiration of all men of good will, whether devout or irreligious.

Where in western civilization is it not present?

One is not surprised to find it throughout Christendom, Judaism's child after the spirit—in Augustine's *City of God*, for example, or Hegel's *Philosophy of History* or Tennyson's allusion to "one far-off divine event."

But, though radically reworked and deeply altered, it can be detected also in so passionate a secularist as Marx, and in innumerable less conspicuous antireligionists who dream to this day of a better world order but know not whence their dream derives.

In the breadth of its diffusion and in the depth of its influence the concept of the Kingdom ranks, next after the Jewish God-faith and ethic, as Israel's largest and most precious gift to mankind.

### 4. MESSIAH

Who will cause the Kingdom latent to become the Kingdom manifest? Who will actualize it?

The Messiah, says the Tradition.

And who is the Messiah?

He is the human being appointed by God and armed by Him with the power and authority to purge the world of its evils and to establish the good upon foundations so firm as never to be moved. He is that descendant of David of whom the prophet spoke when he said:

There shall come forth a shoot out of the stock of Jesse,
And a twig shall grow forth out of his roots.
And the spirit of the Lord shall rest upon him,
The spirit of wisdom and understanding,
The spirit of counsel and might,
The spirit of knowledge and of the fear of the Lord.
And his delight shall be in the fear of the Lord;
And he shall not judge after the sight of his eyes,

Neither decide after the hearing of his ears;
But with righteousness shall he judge the poor,
And decide with equity for the meek of the land;
And he shall smite the land with the rod of his mouth,
And with the breath of his lips shall he slay the wicked.
And righteousness shall be the girdle of his loins,
And faithfulness the girdle of his reins.
And the wolf shall dwell with the lamb,
And the leopard shall lie down with the kid;
And the calf and the young lion and the fatling together;
And a little child shall lead them.
And the cow and the bear shall feed;
Their young ones shall lie down together;
And the lion shall eat straw like the ox.
And the sucking child shall play on the hole of the asp,
And the weaned child shall put his hand on the basilisk's den.
They shall not hurt nor destroy
In all My holy mountain;
For the earth shall be full of the knowledge of the Lord,
As the waters cover the sea.

The Tradition holds then that the world's redemption is to be effected by a single man in one climactic episode.

About this basic faith the Jewish spirit has woven variants innumerable. Some Jews have imagined the Messiah as a mystical superman, others on the other hand as little more than an exceptionally skilled, virtuous, and successful statesman. Indeed, one of the Talmudic sages ventured to suggest that the Messiah had already lived in the time and perhaps in the person of King Hezekiah, but had failed to bring about the universal regeneration expected of him. And no less a personage than Moses ben Nachman, one of the most distinguished of medieval Spanish rabbis, relegated the Messianic doctrine to a secondary position among the articles of Jewish faith.

The Tradition allows then for the widest range of attitudes on the Messiah, including even disbelief, yet the main body of traditionalist opinion is deeply committed to the Messiah-idea and is furthermore quite agreed as to at least some of his major features.

Messiah is always envisaged as a man, even by those who would invest him with extraordinary powers. Never is he supposed to be a God. Again, it is assumed of him that only he can bring lasting deliverance to Israel and the nations.

What then remains for men to do for human redemption? Whatever comes to hand; whatever they can. But with their efforts they must hope, pray, and wait for the Messiah. Only with his aid can victory be won in completeness, the regeneration of men and the transmuting of society being tasks too great for ordinary mortals.

Modernists, to speak paradoxically, believe in a Messianic Age but not in a personal Messiah, not even when he is conceived in the most naturalistic terms. Nor do they doubt the power of mankind to bring the Kingdom into being. The misgivings of the traditionalist on this score, his insistence on help out of the usual, seem to modernists to reflect the conditions of bygone days. In truth ancient or medieval man lived in a universe of which he understood little and controlled less. Very naturally, it never occurred to him to suppose that all unassisted he could remake himself and the world. Wherefore he turned for succor to someone of greater powers than he, someone capable perhaps of the heroic and miraculous.

But man is stronger now. With his growing knowledge of things, his mounting mastery over them, his ever-increasing insight into the workings of his own mind and heart, he is no longer impotent to attain his dreams.

Wherefore, modernists hold, the Messiah is not one man. Rather are all good men messiahs since by laboring together they cause the Kingdom to come. Nor will it arrive all at once. It will be achieved slowly, cumulatively, "precept by precept, line by line, here a little, there a little." Indeed there is a sense in which it will never be altogether achieved, perfection in men and society being a standard to be approximated ever more closely, never however to be matched exactly.

And God, where is He in this process as the modernist envisages it?

He is, as always, at work in men, in their hopes and aspirations, in the skill and fortitude with which they pursue them.

When then the Kingdom has come at last, when the final evil has been broken and the remotest good achieved, the glory of that moment will belong to all the men past and present who have dreamed of it and striven toward it.

But the deeper glory will belong to Him who through the ages has spurred mankind, often against its will, to the greater good and beyond that to the greatest.

In that hour men, departed and living alike, will have abundant reason to chant together the litany of the Psalmist:

"Not unto us, O Lord, not unto us, but unto Thy name give glory."

# EPILOGUE

In medieval Jewish literature there is to be found an exquisite and illuminating parable which, with the slightest adaptation, is admirably suited to stand for everything this book has tried to say.

Once, we are told, a traveler making his way through a difficult and perilous countryside came to the bank of a river too deep to be forded. Return he could not, nor remain where he was. How, then, was he to come to the other side? Then he bethought himself of the purse which dangled from his girdle, containing in the form of gold pieces all his worldly wealth. In the extremity of his need he began to toss the coins one by one into the river, hoping so to raise a pathway for himself over its bed.

In vain! The bag emptied; the river still could not be crossed.

Finally one gold piece remained. Holding this in his hand, the traveler cast about for some other device. Looking here and there he espied a ferry boat far down the river which in his frenzy he had failed to notice earlier. Regretting that he had wasted his treasure to no purpose, yet fortunate in that one coin was left to him for passage money, he hastened to the boat, gave the gold piece to the ferryman and crossed to the other side, so saving his life and going on his way.

Bahya ibn Pakuda, the eleventh century Spanish Jewish moralist who told this tale, had atonement in mind as its point. He was trying to say that penitence ought to be man's first expenditure, but that it proves too often his last—the sole remaining device available to him when all else has been spent.

With no violence to the parable, it can fittingly be applied to the role of religion in life, of Judaism in Israel.

This is the function of faith among men, of the Jewish faith among Jews.

For the wise and the prudent it is the first coin in the purse—that disbursement of the spirit which makes possible the negotiating of life's most dreadful passages—which enables men to go on their way safe and rejoicing.

But for the foolish, the insensitive, the reckless, the undiscerning, it is the last coin in the purse, the one which—when every resource has been exhausted, when man is left with only his need and desperation—purchases a secure crossing to fresh possibilities and new hopes.